Savor

the Brandywine Valley

a Collection of Recipes from
The Junior League of Wilmington, Delaware

The cover photo features the League's
headquarters, the former Lea-Derickson
House along the Brandywine River in
the city of Wilmington. The house was
built in the 1770s with stone from the
north race of the river, and it remained a
private residence until 1960. Mrs.
Charles Reese, Jr., a past-president of
the League, was instrumental in the
1963 preservation of the property. The
house has served as the League's
headquarters since 1965.

Additional copies may be obtained by addressing:

Savor
Junior League of Wilmington, Inc.
1801 N. Market Street
Wilmington, Delaware 19802

or call (302) 652-0544.

Published by   Favorite Recipes® Press
               P.O. Box 305142
               Nashville, Tennessee 37230
               1-800-358-0560

Photography by Bill Deering

LC: 93-070327
ISBN: 0-87197-363-4

First Printing: 1993
Second Printing: 1997

Manufactured in the United States of America

Table of Contents

Acknowledgments

The Junior League of Wilmington wishes to acknowledge those persons without whose help this cookbook would not have been possible.

Mr. Bill Deering, professional photographer, generously contributed his talent, graphically capturing the flavor of the Brandywine Valley.

The cover and layout were designed by Miller Studio, a full-service graphic arts agency in Wilmington, Delaware.

The wine selections were provided by Rita Skelly of King's Wine and Spirits, Wilmington.

The Committee Members who contributed endless time and energy to the completion of the cookbook:

Chairperson: Michelle Wright

Cynthia deLeon

Len deRohan

Julie Diebold

Emily Dryden

Beverley Fleming

Sarah Goudy

Mara Grant

Connie Greendoner

Hazel Kirk

Susan Kremer

Julie Lowe

Jane Martin

Maureen McCollum

Susie Moser

Diane Paul

Jennifer Peterson

Carol Pyle

Mary Rice

Angie Sigmon

Judy Sonnett

Beth Ann Wahl

Kearsley Walsh

Martha White

Diane Wood

Donna Zinnato

History of the League

The Junior League of Wilmington, Inc., celebrates seventy-five years of community service with the release of our cookbook, *Savor the Brandywine Valley: a Collection of Recipes*.

Since its founding in 1918, the League remains committed to improving our community through the effective action of trained volunteers. Members have given of their time, talent and personal resources to initiate projects in response to community needs and to support ongoing programs. Some of our projects, past and present, include:

The Sterck School for the Hearing Impaired

Delaware Curative Workshop

Child Guidance Center

Wilmington Senior Center

Delaware Nature Education Society

Foster Care Review Board

The Ronald McDonald House

Fund-raising projects remain a critical component of our organization. We recognize that quality programs flourish only with adequate funding. The proceeds from *Savor the Brandywine Valley* will help us maintain vital community programs, including the completion of the 75th Anniversary Project, a community playground and garden designed for children, including those with special needs.

The Brandywine Valley

The Brandywine River Valley is a region steeped in American history, rich in cultural institutions and abundant in natural scenic beauty and fragrant gardens. Beginning north of Chadds Ford, Pennsylvania, and reaching southeast through Wilmington to New Castle, Delaware, the area is often described as one of our nation's historic and cultural treasures.

Delaware was an important participant in our nation's colonial past. Caesar Rodney is remembered "as Delaware's own Paul Revere" for his 86-mile horseback ride to Philadelphia in 1776 arriving in time to cast the vote that put Delaware on the side of independence. A statue of Caesar Rodney on horseback is a familiar landmark in the heart of Wilmington's business district.

History comes alive on the picturesque Brandywine Battlefield in Chadds Ford, Pennsylvania, just north of the Delaware state line. On September 10, 1777, the British attacked General Washington's Revolutionary forces. The colonials fought valiantly but could not hold back the enemy. Cannon fire plowed up the ground, and the victors plundered nearby farms of people who had aided General Washington. Today visitors to the 50-acre site can tour the battlefield of one of the costliest defeats of the Revolution.

On December 7, 1787, Delaware was the first of the thirteen states to ratify the United States Constitution, hence the derivation of Delaware's designation as The First State.

The Brandywine River brought commerce to the region. The river valley was the center of the nation's flour-milling industry during and after the Revolutionary War. Later, other industries including the Bancroft textile mills and the gunpowder mills of the fledgling DuPont Company began to thrive due to the dependable power of the river. Commerce flourished along the Brandywine and Wilmington soon became a major port. Today Wilmington is well known for its favorable business climate and the numerous Fortune 500 firms incorporated here, including several of the world's major chemical companies.

The river brought a rich artistic and cultural tradition to the region. Artists felt the Brandywine's elusive appeal and flocked to the valley as a source of inspiration. Its landscapes are simple and gentle, exuding a love for America's past. The commercial resources of the river produced numerous affluent families. Many turned their fortunes to cultural pursuits, becoming patrons of the arts, antiquarians and gardeners on a heroic scale.

Nestled along the banks of the Brandywine in Chadds Ford is the Brandywine River Museum, specializing in American art and home to a large collection of work by the valley's own Wyeth family. In Wilmington, up the hill from the banks of the Brandywine and facing Kentmere Parkway, designed by landscape architect Frederick Olmstead, stands the Delaware Art Museum. The museum houses a superb collection of the work of nineteenth century illustrator Howard Pyle, founder of the Brandywine School of Painting, as well as works by his students Frank Schoonover, N. C. Wyeth and Maxfield Parrish. Thanks to textile industrialist Samuel Bancroft, the museum has the nation's most important gathering of Pre-Raphaelite masterpieces.

No visit to the area is complete without an excursion to both the internationally acclaimed Winterthur Museum and Gardens, home of the country's premier collection of American decorative arts, and Longwood Gardens, a thousand-acre garden paradise.

We hope these photographs and recipes bring a taste of the Brandywine Valley closer to you and that you will come and savor the Brandywine Valley.

A Note about Wine and Food

There are no set rules about what wine to drink with a particular food. To be a true expert, all you need to know is how every wine in the world and every vintage tastes; how every food in the world tastes; and how every food and wine will taste together—obviously not a realistic set of conditions. However, selecting the right wine to enhance your dining experience is not as difficult as it appears. Following are four basic principles that can be used to create successful pairings of food and wine.

1. Sameness. This approach looks for similar characteristics in the wine and foods. The effect should emphasize and enhance those aspects the two have in common. A good example is a full-bodied, oak-aged Chardonnay with a seemingly rich, "buttery" flavor. Such a wine goes well with a rich dish such as chicken cooked in butter and cream since they share the same impressions of flavor.

2. Contrast. The same rich chicken dish described above could be complemented with a crisp, refreshing, lemony flavored wine such as a Sauvignon Blanc. The tartness of the wine "cuts through" the richness of the food leaving the palate refreshed. With the right match, the flavors of the wine take over where the food leaves off, and vice versa, creating a whole new flavor.

3. Equal Intensity. If you don't know in advance what to expect from the particular flavors of a meal, try to match the intensity of the wine to that of the food. If your dish is delicate, choose a delicate wine; if it's robust or intensely flavorful, serve a full-bodied, complex wine. Sometimes it isn't the food that matters but how it is prepared. For example, a simple chicken dish will probably do well with a simple white wine. But if the chicken is charcoal grilled and seasoned with such strong flavors as garlic, rosemary or black pepper, a full-flavored red wine would do it more justice.

4. Personal Preference. This is the most subjective, but potentially most satisfying approach. You are ultimately the expert when it comes to pleasing your palate. Accommodate differing tastes and learn about your own wine preferences by serving two or more wines with dinner. Try them alone and with the food, and then just trust your palate.

In this cookbook, we have suggested wines for most of the entrée dishes. But these suggestions are merely guidelines. Try the wines we've suggested with the dishes you prepare, but also try other varieties that you think might go well, keeping in mind the principles discussed above. We believe that choosing the right wine to complement your meal will improve your whole dining experience.

Rita Skelly and Julie Lowe
King's Wine & Spirits, Wilmington, Delaware

Appetizers

Historic New Castle

Seven miles south of
Wilmington lies New Castle,
Delaware's original state
capital. Stroll the town's
cobblestone streets to find an
impressive display of American
architectural history including
the George Read II house, one
of the great Federal mansions
in America. A nationally
recognized historic area, New
Castle remains much the same
as in its eighteenth and early
nineteenth century golden era.

Baked Brie

Contributed by Anne Nickle

Yield: 15 servings

1 sheet frozen puff pastry, thawed

½ cup slivered almonds, toasted

1 1-pound wheel Brie cheese

1 egg white

Apricot jam to taste (optional)

- Preheat oven to 350 degrees.
- Place pastry sheet on greased baking sheet.
- Sprinkle almonds around center of pastry sheet.
- Place Brie wheel on top of almonds and wrap pastry to completely enclose Brie, trimming off excess pastry. Reserve trimmed pastry.
- Cut leaves, stars or other shapes from reserved pastry for decoration, if desired.
- Turn pastry-wrapped Brie over and decorate with cut-out pastry shapes.
- Brush decorated pastry with egg white.
- Bake for 20 minutes or until brown.
- Drizzle with apricot jam and serve immediately.
- *Note:* Great with water crackers. For an easy variation, place jam on pastry with almonds before wrapping rather than drizzle on top after baking.

Lumpias — Crispy Egg Rolls

Contributed by Barbara McCain

Yield: 50 hors d'oeuvres

2 pounds ground beef

1 pound carrots, grated

1 head celery, finely chopped

2 large green bell peppers, finely chopped

1 bunch scallions, finely chopped

1 head cabbage, grated

1 tablespoon soy sauce

1/2 teaspoon garlic powder

Salt to taste

Pepper to taste

Lemon pepper to taste

50 egg roll sheets

- Brown ground beef in large deep pan.
- Add carrots, celery, green peppers, scallions and cabbage.
- Add soy sauce, garlic powder, salt, pepper and lemon pepper.
- Cover and simmer, stirring occasionally, for 20 minutes or until carrots are tender-crisp.
- Drain excess liquid from pan, taste, and add more seasonings if necessary.
- Place heaping tablespoon of mixture on each egg roll wrapper and roll up according to instructions on egg roll package.
- Deep fry egg rolls until golden brown.
- Serve hot.
- Do not freeze.
- *Note:* Great served with plum sauce for dipping.

Palate Pleasing Crab Balls

Contributed by
Beverley Brainard Fleming

Yield: 24 hors d'oeuvres

1 pound fresh crab meat, not frozen

2 tablespoons finely minced scallions

2 tablespoons Worcestershire sauce

1/8 teaspoon white pepper

1/2 teaspoon salt

2 tablespoons heavy cream

2 hard-boiled eggs, chopped

2 tablespoons finely chopped parsley

2 teaspoons grated lemon rind

1/2 teaspoon garlic salt

1 egg, beaten

Flour for dredging

- Flake and remove shells and membrane from crab meat and place cleaned crab meat in large bowl.
- Add all remaining ingredients except flour to bowl and mix well.
- Chill, covered, for several hours.
- Roll mixture into balls about the size of a quarter, using a measuring tablespoon.
- Roll each ball in flour.
- Preheat oven to 250 degrees.
- Line baking sheet with paper towels.
- Heat oil in deep fryer to 375 degrees.
- Fry balls 4 at a time until golden.
- Place fried balls in oven on paper towels to keep warm until all balls are fried.
- Serve hot or refrigerate for use the next day.
- *Note:* If refrigerated, reheat crab balls in preheated 425-degree oven on wire rack on top of jelly-roll pan for 10 minutes. Can also be frozen on flat surface and then stored in plastic bags. Frozen crab balls should be reheated like refrigerated crab balls, but for 20 minutes rather than 10 minutes.

Yugoslavian Meatballs with Yogurt Dip

Contributed by Michelle Wright

Yield: 100 hors d'oeuvres

4 cups plain yogurt

1 cucumber, peeled, seeded and chopped

6 cloves of garlic, minced, divided

1 tablespoon fresh lemon juice

2 tablespoons olive oil

1/4 teaspoon white pepper

1 tablespoon red wine vinegar

1 pound ground lamb

1 pound ground beef

1 pound ground pork

1 large onion, minced

3 tablespoons paprika

2 tablespoons black pepper

Pinch of fresh nutmeg

- Drain yogurt in cheesecloth in refrigerator overnight.
- Combine yogurt, cucumber, 3 cloves of garlic, lemon juice, olive oil, white pepper and vinegar to make dip. Chill dip until serving time.
- Combine ground meats, onion, remaining garlic, paprika, black pepper and nutmeg.
- Form bite-sized meatballs.
- Cook in small batches on High in microwave for 2 to 3 minutes, or grill for 6 to 8 minutes. Drain.
- Serve with yogurt dip.
- *Note:* An unusual, spicy dish.

Drunken Meatballs

Contributed by Michelle Wright

Yield: 4 dozen

3 pounds lean ground beef or venison

1 large onion, chopped

2 teaspoons chopped parsley

½ teaspoon pepper

½ teaspoon garlic powder

1 teaspoon Worcestershire sauce

1 egg, beaten

¼ cup water

1 14-ounce bottle of catsup

1 12-ounce can beer

- Combine meat, onion, parsley and seasonings.
- Add egg and mix well.
- Form bite-sized meatballs.
- Heat water, catsup and beer in large pot to make sauce.
- Drop meatballs into sauce and boil for 1 hour. Drain off fat.
- Serve meatballs with sauce in chafing dish.

Salami Cornucopias

Contributed by Jane Martin

Yield: 36 hors d'oeuvres

18 paper-thin slices very finely grained large diameter Italian salami

1 pound cream cheese, softened

3 tablespoons minced parsley

3 tablespoons minced chives

3 tablespoons minced dill

Salt to taste

1 teaspoon minced fresh sage (optional)

- Cut each salami slice in half. Twist halves around finger to form cornucopias and press edges together to seal.
- Place cones upright in wire rack or lay carefully on sides on platter.
- Beat cream cheese with remaining ingredients until smooth.
- Pipe cheese mixture into cornucopias using pastry bag fitted with fluted tip.
- Chill, covered, for at least 1 hour before serving.

Stuffed Snow Peas

Contributed by Jane Martin   **Yield: 90 hors d'oeuvres**

2 8-ounce plus 1 3-ounce packages cream cheese, softened

1/2 cup chopped chives

Worcestershire sauce to taste

Salt to taste

White pepper to taste

1 cup cooked salmon, skinned and boned

1 hard-boiled egg, quartered

3 tablespoons Brandy

1 tablespoon butter, softened

1 teaspoon chopped dill

1 teaspoon lemon juice

1 1/2 pounds snow peas

- Blend 16 ounces cream cheese, chives, Worcestershire sauce, salt and pepper in food processor or blender until smooth to make chive filling.
- Purée remaining cream cheese, salmon, egg, Brandy, butter, dill and lemon juice in food processor or blender to make salmon filling.
- Transfer fillings to separate pastry bags fitted with decorative tips.
- Break off ends of snow peas and remove strings.
- Blanch snow peas in enough boiling water to cover for 1 minute.

- Drain snow peas in colander and refresh immediately under cold, running water. Pat snow peas dry with paper towels.
- Slit the stringed side of the snow peas to within 1/4 inch of each end with tip of sharp knife.
- Pipe chive filling into half of the snow peas. Pipe salmon filling into remaining snow peas.
- Arrange on platter and chill, covered, for at least 1 hour.
- *Note:* Cherry tomatoes may be substituted for all or part of the snow peas for a colorful presentation. Cut tops off cherry tomatoes and squeeze out seeds before filling.

Smoked Salmon Canapés

Contributed by Jane Martin

Yield: 40 hors d'oeuvres

¹/₂ cup butter, softened

10 slices thin white bread

Freshly ground black pepper to taste

¹/₂ pound smoked salmon, thinly sliced

- Spread butter on bread slices and sprinkle with pepper.
- Cover with salmon slices.
- Cut canapés with cookie cutters into stars, hearts or any other desired shapes.
- Cover tightly with plastic wrap and chill.
- Serve cold.
- *Note:* An easy, elegant hors d'oeuvre.

Mexican Roll-Ups

Contributed by Karen LeBlond

Yield: 100 hors d'oeuvres

3 8-ounce packages cream cheese, softened

1 8-ounce package shredded Mexican Velveeta cheese

¹/₄ teaspoon chili powder

¹/₄ teaspoon garlic salt

2 small scallions with green tops, chopped

1 10-count package 10-inch flour tortillas

- Cut cream cheese into small chunks and place in large bowl.
- Blend in shredded cheese, chili powder, garlic salt and scallions.
- Spread a thin layer of cheese mixture on each tortilla and roll up tightly.
- Fill ends with cheese mixture when necessary.
- Chill roll-ups on waxed paper, covered with foil, overnight.
- Slice roll-ups into ¹/₂-inch pieces.
- *Note:* Delicious plain or served with salsa.

Broccoli Bread

Contributed by Sandy Pembleton

Yield: 16 servings

1 pound sausage

1   20-ounce package frozen or 1 bunch fresh broccoli, cut into flowerets

2 loaves frozen bread dough, thawed

1 pound mozzarella cheese, shredded

2 tablespoons butter, melted

Garlic salt to taste

- Preheat oven to 350 degrees.
- Crumble sausage into large skillet and cook until browned, stirring frequently.
- Remove sausage from skillet with slotted spoon and place on paper towels.
- Sauté broccoli in sausage drippings. Drain and set aside.
- Roll each bread dough loaf into 8x10-inch rectangle.
- Divide cheese in half and sprinkle, lengthwise, down the center of dough rectangles.
- Sprinkle sausage and broccoli on top of cheese.
- Close each rectangle by bringing together the longer edges, pinching lengthwise seam and two end seams closed.
- Place loaves, seam side down, on lightly greased baking sheet.
- Brush loaves with melted butter and sprinkle with garlic salt.
- Bake for 20 minutes or until golden brown.
- Slice with serrated knife.
- Serve hot.
- *Note:* Spinach can be substituted for broccoli. Can be made ahead, sliced in half if desired, and frozen.

Spinach Pepperoni Frittatas

Contributed by Kearsley Walsh

Yield: 36 hors d'oeuvres

1　10-ounce package frozen spinach, thawed

1½ cups ricotta cheese

¾ cup freshly grated Parmesan cheese

2 eggs

1½ tablespoons Worcestershire sauce

1 teaspoon basil

½ teaspoon salt

½ teaspoon garlic powder

1 teaspoon pepper

½ small onion, finely chopped

8 ounces pepperoni, cut into 36 slices

■ Preheat oven to 375 degrees.

■ Squeeze excess moisture from spinach.

■ Mix spinach, cheeses, eggs, Worcestershire sauce, basil, salt, garlic powder, pepper and onion in large bowl, stirring until blended well.

■ Grease 36 mini-muffin cups or spray cups with nonstick cooking spray.

■ Place one slice of pepperoni in each cup.

■ Top with spinach mixture to fill each cup.

■ Bake for 25 minutes.

■ Serve hot, or cool and remove from cups for freezing.

■ *Note:* If frozen, thaw and reheat at 350 degrees for 10 minutes.

Tabouli

Contributed by Darragh Zehring

Yield: 4 cups

1 cup boiling water

1 cup bulgur wheat

1/2 cup lemon juice

1/2 cup olive oil

2 teaspoons salt

1/4 teaspoon pepper

1 cucumber, peeled, seeded and chopped

1 green bell pepper, seeded and chopped

1/4 cup chopped scallions

1/2 cup chopped parsley

2 tablespoons chopped mint leaves

2 tomatoes, chopped

1 teaspoon sesame oil

- Pour boiling water over bulgur wheat and let stand, covered, for 10 minutes.
- Combine lemon juice, oil, salt and pepper, and mix with bulgur wheat. Chill.
- Add remaining ingredients just before serving.
- *Note:* Serve with chunks of pita bread.

Caviar Pie

Contributed by Judy Miller

Yield: 20 servings

6 hard-boiled eggs, chopped

2 tablespoons mayonnaise

4 scallions with green tops, sliced

Dash of pepper

1 4-ounce jar black caviar

2 cups sour cream

- Combine eggs, mayonnaise, scallions and pepper.
- Spread egg mixture on bottom of 9-inch shallow serving dish.
- Spread caviar over egg mixture.
- Cover caviar with sour cream.
- Refrigerate for at least 4 hours before serving.
- *Note:* Serve with rye or pumpernickel party bread.

Chipped Beef Dip

Contributed by Marnie Rodgers

Yield: 2¹/₂ cups

1 4-ounce package dried beef or chipped beef

8 ounces cream cheese, softened

2 tablespoons milk

¹/₂ cup mayonnaise or combination of mayonnaise and sour cream

¹/₂ cup chopped pecans

Salt to taste

Pepper to taste

4 scallions, chopped

- Preheat oven to 350 degrees.
- Combine all ingredients and blend well.
- Just before serving, bake, covered, for 20 to 25 minutes.
- Serve warm. Do not reheat.
- *Note:* Serve with crackers.

Nacho Dip

Contributed by Linda McLeary

Yield: 6 cups

1 pound lean ground beef

1 pound sweet or hot Italian sausage

½ small onion, chopped

1   10-ounce can cream of mushroom soup

1 cup taco sauce or salsa (see "Fresh Salsa" in the Restaurant Section)

8 ounces Velveeta cheese

8 ounces Mexican Velveeta cheese

- Preheat oven to 350 degrees.
- Brown ground beef, sausage and onion in large skillet. Drain thoroughly.
- Add mushroom soup and taco sauce to skillet and blend well.
- Transfer mixture to 3-quart casserole dish.
- Slice cheeses and stir into casserole dish.
- Bake for 30 minutes or until cheese is melted.
- Remove from oven and skim off any fat that has risen to top of dish.
- Stir well and serve warm with taco chips.
- *Note:* A hearty dip that men love. Can be frozen and reheated in microwave.

Crowd Pleasin' Chutney Spread

Contributed by Becky Hamlin

Yield: 2¹/₂ cups

2 8-ounce packages light cream cheese, softened

3 tablespoons curry powder

1 teaspoon salt

1 6-ounce jar ginger chutney

2 bunches scallions, sliced

10 strips bacon, cooked and crumbled

¹/₄ cup finely chopped smoked almonds or sesame seeds

- Blend cream cheese, curry powder and salt.
- Spread cheese mixture on bottom of 10-inch quiche dish.
- Purée chutney in food processor or blender.
- Spread chutney on top of cheese mixture.
- Spread scallions evenly over chutney layer, followed by bacon and almonds.
- *Note:* Serve with Melba toast or wheat crackers. May be prepared a day ahead.

Tsatziki — Greek Garlic Dip

Contributed by Michelle Wright

Yield: 3 cups

32 ounces plain yogurt

2 tablespoons olive oil

2 tablespoons red wine vinegar

2 to 3 cloves of garlic, minced

¹/₄ teaspoon white pepper

1 cucumber, peeled, seeded and diced

1 tablespoon minced fresh dill

- Drain yogurt in cheesecloth overnight in refrigerator.
- Combine oil, vinegar, garlic and pepper in large bowl and mix thoroughly.
- Add yogurt and cucumber.
- Chill.
- Sprinkle with dill just before serving.
- *Note:* Serve with chunks of pita or French bread. Garnish serving dish with slices of cucumber or radishes.

Hummus

Contributed by Connie Greendoner

Yield: 1 1/2 cups

1   1-pound can chick-peas or
    garbanzo beans

2 cloves of garlic

Juice of 1 lemon

2 tablespoons tahini (sesame
  seed paste)

2 tablespoons olive oil

1/2 teaspoon salt

1/8 teaspoon pepper

1/2 teaspoon cumin

- Drain chick-peas and reserve liquid.
- Pour chick-peas into food processor.
- Turn on processor and add garlic, lemon juice, tahini, oil, salt, pepper and cumin.
- Add reserved liquid from chick-peas slowly until mixture reaches desired consistency.
- Process until very smooth.
- *Note:* Serve with chunks of pita bread or tortilla chips.

Clam Dip

Contributed by Lisa Humphreys

Yield: 3 cups

2   7-ounce cans minced clams

2   8-ounce packages cream
    cheese, softened

1 small onion, minced

1 teaspoon mayonnaise

1 teaspoon lemon juice

1 1/2 tablespoons
    Worcestershire sauce

2 drops of Tabasco sauce

- Drain clams and reserve juice.
- Combine cream cheese, clams and enough reserved juice to reach desired consistency.
- Add onion, mayonnaise, lemon juice, Worcestershire sauce and Tabasco sauce to clam mixture.
- *Note:* An excellent dip with corn chips or crackers.

Shrimp Parfaits

Contributed by Jane Martin

Yield: 10 servings

2¹/₂ pounds small raw shrimp

1¹/₄ cups Green Mayonnaise (recipe follows) or mayonnaise

¹/₄ cup light cream

1 small head Boston or other soft lettuce, shredded

¹/₂ cup pimento strips

5 hard-boiled eggs, sieved

¹/₂ cup capers

10 sprigs of watercress or dill

10 lemon slices

- Rinse shrimp and place in large saucepan. Add cold water to cover shrimp by 1 inch, and bring to a boil over moderately low heat.
- Remove pan from heat and drain shrimp in colander.
- Let shrimp stand until cool enough to handle. Peel and devein shrimp and chill, covered.
- Mix mayonnaise and cream.
- Line bottom of 10 parfait glasses with shredded lettuce.
- Fill glasses with alternating layers of shrimp, mayonnaise mixture, pimento, eggs, lettuce and capers.
- Top each of the parfaits with 1 or 2 shrimp, a sprig of watercress or dill and a lemon slice.
- Serve cold.
- *Note:* A cool and elegant first course.

Green Mayonnaise

2 tablespoons each finely chopped parsley, dill, chives and watercress

2 hard-boiled egg yolks

1 cup mayonnaise

- Blanch herbs for 2 minutes and drain well.
- Place herbs and egg yolks in food processor or blender and process to a paste.
- Stir herb paste into mayonnaise.

Appetizers

See also...

- Fresh Salsa
- Hot Crab Dip
- Shiitake and Smoked Salmon Canapés
- Stuffed Mushrooms à la Grècque

...in the Restaurant Section

Soups ▪ *Salads* ▪ *Breads*

The Brandywine River

Throughout the city of
Wilmington one can find
many scenic and
recreational parks where
residents and visitors can
enjoy canoeing, hiking and
nature walks. An effort
has been initiated to
expand and preserve a
"Green Way" so that all
may continue to enjoy the
beauty of the river valley.
Pictured is the river near
the Brandywine Zoo in
Wilmington.

Avocado Bisque

Contributed by Scott Daniels   **Yield: 4 servings**

1 large ripe avocado, peeled and seeded

1 tablespoon fresh lemon juice

Juice of 1 lime

1 cup chicken broth

1 cup heavy cream

2 tablespoons sliced scallions

1 tablespoon chopped fresh chives, divided

Salt and pepper to taste

- Combine all ingredients except pepper and 1 teaspoon chives in blender or food processor and process until coarsely blended, but do not purée.
- Chill until ready to serve.
- Garnish with remaining chives and pepper.

Mushroom Chive Bisque

Contributed by Julie Lowe   **Yield: 6 servings**

3/4 cup butter

1 pound mushrooms, sliced

6 tablespoons all-purpose flour

3/8 teaspoon dry mustard

1/2 teaspoon salt

3 cups chicken broth

2 cups half and half

1/4 cup Sherry

1/4 cup chopped fresh or dried chives

1/4 cup whipping cream, whipped (optional)

- Melt butter in large saucepan and sauté mushrooms. Do not overcook.
- Add flour, mustard and salt to saucepan and cook for 1 minute.
- Add broth and cook over medium-high heat until thickened, but do not boil.
- Add half and half, Sherry and chives and heat to serving temperature. Do not boil.
- Float whipped cream on top.
- *Note:* To serve cold, process all ingredients except whipping cream in blender then chill. Serve topped with whipped cream.

Carrot Chowder

Contributed by Mady Jaquin

Yield: 6 servings

1 pound ground beef

1/2 teaspoon salt

1/2 cup chopped celery

1/2 cup chopped onion

1/2 cup diced green bell pepper

4 cups tomato juice

1 1/2 cups water

2   10-ounce cans cream of
   celery soup

2 1/2 cups grated carrots

1 teaspoon sugar

1/2 teaspoon garlic salt or
   3 cloves of garlic, minced

1/2 teaspoon pepper

1/8 teaspoon marjoram

6 slices Swiss cheese

- Brown ground beef in skillet and drain.
- Add salt, celery, onion and green pepper to skillet.
- Cover and simmer over low heat until vegetables are tender, about 10 minutes.
- Combine tomato juice, water, celery soup, carrots, sugar, garlic salt, pepper and marjoram in large saucepan.
- Add beef mixture to saucepan.
- Simmer for 30 minutes.
- Place cheese slices in individual bowls.
- Top with hot chowder.
- *Note:* Other sliced cheeses can be substituted.

Curried Carrot Soup

Contributed by Carol Lennig

Yield: 6 servings

1/4 cup butter or margarine

1 large onion, chopped

1 pound carrots, pared and sliced

3/4 teaspoon curry powder

1 thin slice lemon peel

1 quart chicken broth

1 1/2 teaspoons salt

1/4 teaspoon pepper

1 cup light cream

- Melt butter in large saucepan.
- Sauté onion and carrots in butter for about 5 minutes or until onion is tender.
- Add curry powder and lemon peel to vegetable mixture and cook for 3 minutes more.
- Add chicken broth to saucepan and bring to a boil.
- Lower heat and simmer, covered, for about 20 minutes or until carrots are tender.
- Remove saucepan from heat and let cool slightly.
- Purée soup in batches in food processor or blender until smooth.
- Pour puréed soup into large bowl and stir in salt, pepper and cream.
- Cover bowl and chill for at least 4 hours.
- *Note:* Milk or low-fat milk can be substituted for cream, but use less so that soup is not too thin.

Cauliflower and Corn Soup

Contributed by Michelle Wright

Yield: 8 servings

1 medium white onion, chopped

2 tablespoons butter or margarine

2 tablespoons all-purpose flour

2½ cups chicken broth

2 cups fresh cauliflowerets

1 cup milk

¼ cup half and half

Cayenne pepper to taste

1 cup cooked corn

1 tablespoon minced fresh parsley

- Sauté onion in butter in large pot until soft and almost transparent.
- Stir in flour and cook for 3 minutes, stirring constantly.
- Add broth and stir with whisk until smooth.
- Add cauliflower and cook, covered, on low heat for 30 minutes.
- Purée cauliflower in pot with potato masher, or in blender and return to pot.
- Add milk, half and half and cayenne pepper.
- Add cooked corn and heat through, but do not boil.
- Garnish with parsley and serve hot.

Potato Sausage and Cheese Soup

Contributed by Julie Lowe

Yield: 10 servings

1 pound hot sausage

5 medium-sized potatoes, peeled and chopped

2 medium-sized onions, chopped

1/4 cup butter

1/4 cup all-purpose flour

2 cups milk

1 cup heavy cream

2 cups grated sharp Cheddar cheese

1 tablespoon chopped parsley

Salt and pepper to taste

- Brown sausage in skillet. Drain and chop into bite-sized pieces. Set aside.
- Place potatoes and onions in large pot with enough water to cover and boil until tender. Do not drain.
- Melt butter in saucepan, add flour, mix and cook for 1 minute.
- Add milk to saucepan gradually and cook until mixture thickens to make cream sauce, stirring constantly.
- Add cream sauce and sausage to potato mixture.
- Stir in heavy cream, cheese, parsley, salt and pepper and heat thoroughly, but do not boil.
- *Note:* This cheesy, hearty soup may be prepared in less than an hour. Any sausage can be used, but it is best with hot breakfast or country sausage.

Swiss Potato Soup

Contributed by Michelle Wright

Yield: 24 servings

1 pound bacon, chopped

1 pound onions, chopped

½ bunch green onions, chopped

1 head green cabbage, chopped

72 ounces chicken broth

4 ounces dry white wine (optional)

3 pounds potatoes, peeled and halved

12 ounces Gruyère cheese, grated

1½ cups heavy cream

White pepper to taste

- Sauté bacon in large pot until brown and crisp.
- Add onions, green onions and cabbage to pot and sauté for 8 to 10 minutes or until vegetables are soft.
- Add chicken broth, wine and potatoes to pot and simmer for 40 minutes or until potatoes are very tender.
- Add grated cheese gradually, stirring until cheese melts.
- Stir in cream and pepper and heat, but do not boil.

Sweet Potato Vichyssoise

Contributed by a Friend

Yield: 8 servings

1³/₄ cups sliced scallions

5 cups chicken broth, divided

2¹/₂ pounds sweet potatoes, baked

Salt and pepper to taste

¹/₂ cup half and half

Chopped chives to taste

- Combine scallions and 1 cup chicken broth in large saucepan and simmer until scallions are tender, approximately 15 minutes.
- Scoop out pulp from sweet potatoes. Discard skins.
- Purée sweet potato pulp with scallion mixture in blender until smooth.
- Transfer purée to saucepan, add remaining chicken broth and simmer for 5 minutes.
- Add salt and pepper to soup and remove from heat.
- Let soup cool and place in refrigerator to chill.
- Stir half and half into chilled mixture when ready to serve. Garnish with chives.
- *Note:* Evaporated skim milk can be substituted for half and half to reduce fat.

Wild Rice Soup

Contributed by a Friend

Yield: 4 servings

4 cups duck or beef broth,
  homemade or canned

1 onion, chopped

1 cup chopped celery

1 large carrot, chopped

1 teaspoon peppercorns

1/2 teaspoon thyme

1/2 teaspoon parsley

1 bay leaf

1/2 cup wild rice, uncooked

2 cups water

1/4 cup butter, softened

1/4 cup all-purpose flour

1/2 cup heavy cream

Salt and pepper to taste

- Combine broth, onion, celery, carrot, peppercorns, thyme, parsley and bay leaf in large pot and bring to a boil.
- Simmer over medium heat for 15 minutes.
- Cook rice in 2 cups water in separate saucepan for about 1/2 hour or until tender and drain.
- Strain soup and discard vegetables. Return soup to large pot.
- Combine butter and flour and mix until smooth.
- Add butter mixture to soup and whisk constantly until well blended.
- Cook over medium heat, stirring often, until soup thickens.
- Add rice and continue to simmer for 20 minutes.
- Stir in cream, but do not boil.
- Season with salt and pepper.

Hearty Meatball Soup

Contributed by Sandy Pembleton　　　**Yield: 6 servings**

1½ pounds ground beef

1 egg

½ cup bread crumbs

5 tablespoons chopped parsley

2 tablespoons margarine

2 cups water

1　10-ounce can condensed beef broth

1　1-pound 12-ounce can tomatoes, undrained

1　1-ounce package dry onion soup mix

2 cups sliced carrots

¼ cup chopped celery

¼ teaspoon pepper

¼ teaspoon oregano

¼ teaspoon basil

1 bay leaf

- Combine ground beef, egg, bread crumbs and parsley in large bowl.
- Form beef mixture into bite-sized meatballs.
- Sauté meatballs in margarine in large skillet until lightly browned. Drain meatballs and set aside.
- Combine water, beef broth, tomatoes, onion soup mix, carrots, celery and remaining seasonings in large deep saucepan and boil for 30 minutes.
- Add meatballs to broth mixture and cook for 20 minutes more, or place broth and meatballs in slow-cooker and cook according to slow-cooker instructions.
- *Note:* This hearty soup, served with salad and crusty bread, makes a great winter meal.

Zesty Italian Soup

Contributed by Julie Lowe

Yield: 8 servings

1 pound Italian sausage
(¹/₂ pound hot sausage and
¹/₂ pound sweet sausage)

2 cups bite-sized slices celery

2 pounds zucchini, sliced into
¹/₂-inch pieces

1 cup chopped onion

2 28-ounce cans whole
tomatoes, plus 1 tomato can
water (or 4 pounds fresh
tomatoes, peeled and cut
into eighths, plus
1¹/₂ cups tomato juice)

2 teaspoons salt

1 teaspoon oregano

1 teaspoon Italian seasoning

¹/₄ teaspoon garlic powder

1 teaspoon sugar

¹/₂ teaspoon basil

2 green bell peppers, cut into
¹/₂-inch pieces

- Brown sausage in large pan and drain excess fat.
- Add celery to sausage and cook for 10 minutes, stirring occasionally.
- Add all remaining ingredients except green peppers.
- Simmer, covered, for 20 minutes.
- Add green peppers, cover and simmer for 10 minutes more.
- *Note:* This is a great soup meal for a cold winter day. Serve soup with garlic bread and grated Parmesan cheese. Spiciness can be varied by using any combination of hot, sweet or mild sausage.

Quick Chicken Tortellini Soup

Contributed by Cynthia deLeon

Yield: 8 servings

72 ounces chicken broth

1   14-ounce package frozen cheese tortellini

1   16-ounce package frozen stir-fried vegetables

2 whole chicken breasts, cooked, boned and cut into bite-sized pieces

- Boil broth in large pot. Add tortellini and cook according to package instructions.
- Add vegetables to pot and cook until heated through.
- Add chicken to pot and serve.

Easy Crab Soup

Contributed by Sharon Reuter

Yield: 8 servings

2   10-ounce cans cream of mushroom soup

2   10-ounce cans cream of asparagus soup

1 soup can milk

1 pound crab meat

1/2 cup dry white wine

- Combine soups, milk and crab meat in large saucepan.
- Mix well over low to medium heat until warm.
- Add wine and reheat before serving.

Pink Gazpacho

Contributed by Nancy Albright

Yield: 4 servings

1 cup beef broth

2 cups chopped tomatoes

1/2 cup sliced beets

1/2 cup chopped green bell pepper

1/4 cup chopped celery

3 tablespoons chopped onion

1 clove of garlic, chopped

1 teaspoon salt

1/8 teaspoon Tabasco sauce

1 tablespoon paprika

1/2 teaspoon basil

1/4 cup red wine vinegar

1/4 cup olive oil

1/2 cup chopped, seeded cucumber

- Combine beef broth and tomatoes in blender.
- Add all remaining ingredients except cucumber and blend thoroughly.
- Chill.
- Garnish with chopped cucumber.
- *Note:* This soup is refreshing, spicy and a beautiful deep pink color.

Chunky Gazpacho

Contributed by Janet Lemons,
Doris Kremer

1 clove of garlic, halved

6 large ripe tomatoes, peeled, seeded and chopped

1 red bell pepper, chopped

1 green bell pepper, chopped

2 medium-sized onions, chopped

2 large cucumbers, peeled, seeded and chopped

1/2 cup olive oil

1/4 cup lemon juice

2 cups tomato juice

1 tablespoon Worcestershire sauce

Salt and pepper to taste

Tabasco sauce to taste

1/2 cup chopped fresh herbs (chives, parsley, basil, chervil, tarragon...your choice)

Yield: 8 servings

- Rub large bowl with garlic and discard garlic.
- Combine tomatoes, peppers, onions and cucumbers in bowl.
- Mix oil, lemon juice and tomato juice and pour over vegetables.
- Stir Worcestershire sauce, salt, pepper, Tabasco sauce and herbs into vegetable mixture.
- Cover bowl and chill for at least 4 hours.
- *Note:* Garnish with lemon or lime slices, croutons or sour cream.

Apple Beet Salad

Contributed by Hebba Lund

Yield: 4 servings

1   16-ounce jar of pickled
     Harvard beets

2 Granny Smith apples,
   peeled and diced

2 tablespoons mayonnaise

Chopped fresh parsley to taste

- Combine beets and apples in large bowl.
- Stir in mayonnaise and chill.
- Sprinkle with parsley before serving.

Arugula Avocado Salad

Contributed by a Friend

Yield: 6 servings

6 sun-dried tomatoes, in oil

1 tablespoon tarragon vinegar
  or red wine vinegar

Pinch of thyme

Pinch of marjoram

1 tablespoon fresh tarragon

Salt and pepper to taste

4 bunches arugula, trimmed
  and broken into pieces

1 small ripe avocado, chunked

- Drain tomatoes and reserve oil.
- Mix vinegar, tomatoes, herbs and 4 tablespoons reserved oil in blender to make dressing.
- Add salt and pepper to dressing.
- Combine arugula and avocado in bowl and toss with dressing.
- *Note:* Watercress may be substituted for arugula.

Artichoke Rice Salad

Contributed by Kathy Segars

Yield: 8 servings

1   5-ounce package chicken-flavored seasoned rice mix

15 green olives, sliced

4 scallions, chopped

½ cup chopped red bell pepper

2   8-ounce jars marinated artichoke hearts, drained and quartered

½ cup mayonnaise

1 teaspoon curry powder

- Cook rice mix according to package instructions and cool.
- Add olives, scallions, red pepper and artichoke hearts to rice.
- Combine mayonnaise and curry powder.
- Add mayonnaise mixture to rice and mix well.
- Chill for at least 4 hours before serving.
- *Note:* This dish is also great served as a main course on a hot summer day.

Butter Bean Salad

Contributed by Michelle Wright, Nancy Graves

Yield: 6 servings

2   15-ounce cans butter beans, rinsed and drained

2 tablespoons olive oil

⅓ cup freshly squeezed lemon juice

½ cup minced parsley

½ cup thinly sliced onions

2 large tomatoes, seeded, cored and diced

1 teaspoon pepper

⅓ cup feta cheese

- Mix beans, oil, lemon juice, parsley, onions, tomatoes and pepper in large bowl.
- Cover and chill for 4 hours.
- Crumble cheese onto salad just before serving.
- *Note:* Chick-peas may be substituted for all or part of the butter beans.

Oriental Cabbage Salad

Contributed by Michelle Wright

Yield: 6 servings

1   3-ounce package oriental noodles with chicken-flavored seasoning packet

½ cup boiling water

4 cups shredded cabbage

¼ cup sliced green onions

2 tablespoons sesame seed

3 tablespoons red wine vinegar

2 tablespoons sugar

2 tablespoons olive oil

½ teaspoon ground white pepper

½ cup slivered almonds, toasted

- Crush noodles slightly and place in medium-sized bowl.
- Pour boiling water over noodles to soften.
- Let stand for 5 minutes. Drain well in colander.
- Combine softened noodles, cabbage, onions and sesame seed in large bowl.
- Combine seasoning packet from noodle package, vinegar, sugar, oil and white pepper in blender and blend well.
- Pour seasoning mixture over noodle mixture and toss.
- Cover and chill for at least 4 hours.
- Stir in toasted almonds just before serving.

Do-Ahead Cabbage Salad

Contributed by Sandy Pembleton

Yield: 8 servings

1 head cabbage

1 red bell pepper

1 green bell pepper

2 carrots

1 tablespoon salt

2 cups sugar

1 cup vinegar

¼ cup water

1 teaspoon celery seed

- Chop or grate cabbage, peppers and carrots by hand or in food processor.
- Place vegetables in large bowl.
- Add salt and mix thoroughly.
- Let stand for 1 hour. Drain mixture.
- Combine sugar, vinegar, water and celery seed in medium saucepan. Bring to a boil and continue boiling for 3 minutes.
- Pour hot liquid over cabbage mixture.
- Let cool.
- Put mixture in 1 large or several small freezer containers and freeze.
- Thaw before serving.
- Serve cold.
- *Note:* Good do-ahead salad for picnics.

Apple Coleslaw

Contributed by Sunny McGeorge

Yield: 8 servings

2 cups plain yogurt

1 cup sour cream

2²/₃ tablespoons honey

7 cups shredded red cabbage

4 Granny Smith apples,
   peeled and chopped

²/₃ cup finely minced onion

³/₄ cup chopped parsley

Salt and pepper to taste

- Combine yogurt, sour cream and honey in large bowl.
- Add cabbage, apples, onion and parsley and stir.
- Add salt and pepper and mix well.
- Refrigerate for 2 to 4 hours before serving.
- *Note:* A delicious way to add color to a summer meal.

Cucumber Slaw

Contributed by Virginia Wood

Yield: 8 servings

2 cucumbers

1 teaspoon salt

2 to 3 tablespoons sugar

2 to 3 tablespoons white
   vinegar

2 tablespoons mayonnaise

1 small red onion, finely
   chopped

- Peel cucumbers and slice very thinly.
- Mix salt, sugar, vinegar and mayonnaise in medium bowl.
- Add cucumbers and onion to bowl and toss well.
- Refrigerate for at least 1 hour before serving.

Honey Mustard Coleslaw

Contributed by Michelle Wright

Yield: 8 servings

3/4 cup mayonnaise

1 tablespoon honey

2 teaspoons Dijon mustard

6 cups shredded cabbage

2 cups shredded carrots

6 radishes, chopped

- Combine mayonnaise, honey and mustard, and mix until blended to form dressing.
- Combine cabbage, carrots and radishes in large bowl.
- Add dressing to vegetable mixture and toss.
- Chill before serving.

Cauliflower and Broccoli Salad

Contributed by Audrey Buckalew

Yield: 10 servings

1 head cauliflower, cut into flowerets

2 bunches broccoli, cut into flowerets

1 medium red onion, finely chopped

8 strips bacon

3/4 cup raisins

1 cup mayonnaise

1/2 cup sugar

1 tablespoon white wine vinegar

- Combine cauliflower, broccoli and onion in large bowl.
- Fry bacon until crisp. Drain on paper towels.
- Crumble bacon and add to vegetables.
- Add raisins and mix well.
- Combine mayonnaise, sugar and vinegar and stir well to make dressing.
- Pour dressing over salad and toss thoroughly.
- Refrigerate until serving time.

Hearts of Palm Salad

Contributed by a Friend

Yield: 4 servings

1/4 cup red raspberry or red wine vinegar

1 tablespoon mustard

Salt and pepper to taste

1/2 cup peanut or olive oil

1/4 cup Champagne

1   12-ounce can hearts of palm, cut into 1-inch pieces

1   12-ounce can small black olives

1/2 cup chopped red onion

1 hard-boiled egg, sliced

2 teaspoons fresh or 1/2 teaspoon dried dill

■ Combine vinegar, mustard, salt and pepper in small bowl with wire whisk.

■ Blend oil, then Champagne, into vinegar mixture gradually, whisking constantly.

■ Arrange hearts of palm, olives, onion and egg slices on individual serving plates.

■ Pour dressing over top of each serving and sprinkle with dill.

■ *Note:* Equal parts of white wine and sparkling water may be substituted for Champagne.

Garlicky Green Salad

Contributed by Linda Miller

Yield: 8 servings

2 heads Bibb lettuce or
   1 large head red leaf lettuce

$1/2$ cup walnuts, coarsely
   chopped

5 tablespoons walnut oil,
   divided

$1/2$ teaspoon basil

$1/2$ teaspoon rosemary

$1/2$ cup vegetable oil

3 tablespoons white wine
   vinegar

3 cloves of garlic, chopped

Salt to taste

Coarsely ground black pepper
   to taste

1 cup Parmesan cheese

- Tear lettuce into bite-sized pieces.
- Sauté walnuts in 1 tablespoon walnut oil mixed with basil and rosemary in skillet until toasted to taste. Let cool and set aside.
- Combine remaining walnut oil, vegetable oil, vinegar, garlic, salt and pepper to make dressing.
- Toss lettuce, walnuts, dressing and cheese in large bowl.
- Serve immediately.

Five Minute Caesar Salad

Contributed by Pattie Thurston   **Yield: 8 servings**

3 heads romaine lettuce

1 teaspoon garlic salt

1 tablespoon red wine vinegar

1 egg

3 tablespoons olive oil

1 tablespoon Worcestershire sauce

2 tablespoons lemon juice

2 teaspoons Dijon mustard

Freshly ground black pepper to taste

1/4 cup grated Parmesan or Locatelli cheese

1 cup croutons

- Wash lettuce, dry thoroughly, and break into large, bite-sized pieces. Set aside.
- Sprinkle garlic salt around bottom of large bowl.
- Add vinegar and egg to bowl and mix well.
- Blend in olive oil thoroughly.
- Add Worcestershire sauce, lemon juice, mustard and pepper, and mix well.
- Add lettuce pieces to bowl and toss.
- Add grated cheese and croutons.
- Toss again, making sure lettuce is coated well with dressing.
- Serve immediately.
- *Note:* An additional 1 tablespoon mustard may be substituted for the egg.

Overnight Salad

Contributed by Marnie Rodgers

Yield: 10 servings

1 head iceberg lettuce, shredded

3 celery stalks, chopped

1 green bell pepper, chopped

1 large white onion, chopped

1   10-ounce package frozen peas

1 teaspoon sugar

3/4 cup mayonnaise

1/2 pound Cheddar cheese, grated

6 strips bacon, cooked and crumbled

- Layer ingredients in order in large glass serving dish or salad bowl
- Refrigerate for at least 8 hours to overnight.
- Toss immediately before serving.

Spaghetti Salad

Contributed by Kim Simpson

Yield: 8 servings

1   1-pound box spaghetti

1   8-ounce bottle of Italian dressing

1   1-ounce package dry Italian dressing mix

2 medium-sized Vidalia onions or 2 bunches scallions, chopped

3 large tomatoes, seeded and chopped

2 green bell peppers, chopped

1 teaspoon oregano

- Cook spaghetti according to package instructions and drain.
- Place spaghetti in large bowl.
- Combine Italian dressing and dry dressing mix.
- Pour over spaghetti and toss.
- Combine onions, tomatoes, peppers and oregano.
- Add to spaghetti and toss lightly.
- Chill.

Layered Walnut Salad

Contributed by Linda Shaffer

Yield: 10 servings

1 cup walnuts

1 teaspoon salad oil

¼ teaspoon garlic salt

⅛ teaspoon dill

4 cups finely shredded
  iceberg lettuce, divided

8 cherry tomatoes, halved

1 cup shredded Cheddar
  cheese

1 10-ounce package frozen
  peas, thawed and drained

½ cup sour cream

¾ cup mayonnaise

1 tablespoon lemon juice

1 teaspoon prepared mustard

½ teaspoon salt

2 tablespoons chopped green
  onions

2 teaspoons chopped parsley

- Preheat oven to 350 degrees.
- Drop walnuts into rapidly boiling water, boil for 3 minutes and drain.
- Toss walnuts with oil, garlic salt and dill, and place on shallow baking pan in single layer.
- Toast walnuts in oven for 10 to 12 minutes, stirring once. Let cool.
- Place 2 cups lettuce in bottom of straight-sided glass salad bowl.
- Add tomatoes to bowl, placing cut sides against glass, facing out.
- Layer cheese, peas, ¾ cup toasted walnuts and remaining lettuce in bowl.
- Combine remaining ingredients to make dressing. Spread 1 cup of dressing over salad, spreading to edges of bowl. Refrigerate remaining dressing.
- Cover salad bowl and chill for several hours to overnight.
- Top salad with remaining dressing and walnuts before serving.

Broccoli-Mushroom Salad

Contributed by Charlene Bertheaud

Yield: 8 servings

¹/₄ cup sugar

1 teaspoon paprika

1 teaspoon celery seed

1 teaspoon salt

1 cup olive oil

¹/₄ cup wine vinegar

1 pound fresh broccoli, cut into bite-sized flowerets

1 pound fresh mushrooms, sliced

2 bunches scallions, sliced

- Mix sugar, paprika, celery seed, salt, oil and vinegar to make dressing.
- Chill dressing for 1 hour.
- Combine broccoli, mushrooms and scallions in large salad bowl.
- Pour dressing over the vegetables and toss well.
- Chill for 30 minutes before serving.

Pickled Mushroom Salad

Contributed by Joan Chalfant

Yield: 6 servings

¹/₃ cup red wine vinegar

¹/₃ cup salad oil

1 small onion, thinly sliced

1 teaspoon salt

2 tablespoons chopped parsley

1 teaspoon Dijon mustard

1 tablespoon packed brown sugar

1 pound mushrooms

6 large leaves lettuce

- Combine all ingredients except mushrooms and lettuce in large saucepan.
- Bring mixture to a boil.
- Add mushrooms and simmer for 5 minutes.
- Chill overnight.
- Drain and serve over lettuce leaves.

Pea Salad with Smoked Almonds

Contributed by Diane Bold

Yield: 6 servings

1/4 cup mayonnaise

1/4 teaspoon curry powder

1 clove of garlic, finely minced

1   16-ounce package frozen peas

1   6-ounce can smoked almonds

- Combine mayonnaise, curry powder and garlic in medium bowl.
- Add frozen peas and toss.
- Refrigerate for 12 hours to overnight.
- Add smoked almonds just before serving and toss well.
- *Note:* A delicious, unusual cold side dish for a hot summer night.

Pepper Salad

Contributed by Diane Bold

Yield: 4 servings

1 1/2 tablespoons olive oil

2 tablespoons balsamic vinegar

1/4 teaspoon rosemary

Freshly ground pepper to taste

1 red bell pepper, chopped

1 yellow bell pepper, chopped

1 green bell pepper, chopped

- Beat oil and vinegar in large bowl.
- Add rosemary and ground pepper and stir.
- Stir in chopped peppers and mix well.

Mama's Potato Salad

Contributed by a Friend

Yield: 6 servings

6 medium-sized potatoes

6 hard-boiled eggs

½ cup chopped onion or scallions

½ cup chopped celery

½ cup chopped green bell pepper

1 cup mayonnaise

2 tablespoons pickle relish

1 teaspoon caraway seed

Salt and pepper to taste

■ Boil potatoes, drain, peel and set aside to cool.

■ Slice eggs and potatoes and combine with chopped vegetables in large bowl.

■ Add mayonnaise, relish and caraway seed. Toss gently.

■ Add salt and pepper.

■ Refrigerate until served.

■ *Note:* Best when made a day in advance.

Macaroni Salad

Contributed by Harriott Kimmel

Yield: 12 servings

1 pound elbow macaroni

1 tablespoon tarragon vinegar

1 tablespoon red wine vinegar

1/4 teaspoon rosemary

1/4 teaspoon minced garlic

Salt and pepper to taste

1/4 cup vegetable oil

1 1/2 tablespoons olive oil

1 tablespoon hot water

1 1/2 cups mayonnaise

1 cup diced cooked ham

1 cup sliced scallions

1 tablespoon Dijon mustard

- Cook macaroni according to package instructions, drain and keep warm.
- Combine tarragon vinegar, red wine vinegar, rosemary, garlic, salt and pepper in bowl of electric mixer.
- Turn on mixer and add oils in steady stream while mixer is running to make dressing.
- Add hot water to dressing and beat for 5 minutes.
- Pour dressing over warm macaroni and toss.
- Add mayonnaise, ham, scallions and mustard and toss until well mixed.
- Season with salt and pepper to taste.
- Serve immediately, or refrigerate overnight and bring to room temperature before serving.
- *Note:* Garnish with sliced hard-boiled eggs, ripe olives and additional diced ham.

Pasta Primavera Salad

Contributed by Julie Lowe

Yield: 8 servings

4 asparagus spears, cut into 1-inch pieces

½ pound zucchini, sliced

1 cup broccoli flowerets

½ cup fresh or frozen green peas

¼ pound mushrooms, sliced

2 tomatoes, seeded and chopped coarsely

½ pound spaghetti or linguine

3 tablespoons chopped fresh or 1 tablespoon dried basil

¼ cup chopped fresh or 2 tablespoons dried parsley

1½ cups mayonnaise

2 teaspoons minced garlic

2 tablespoons white vinegar

Salt and pepper to taste

- Cook asparagus in boiling water or microwave until tender-crisp.
- Drain asparagus in colander and refresh under cold running water. Drain well and set aside.
- Repeat with zucchini, broccoli and peas separately.
- Combine cooked vegetables, mushrooms and tomatoes in large bowl.
- Break spaghetti strands in half. Cook according to package instructions and drain.
- Rinse cooked spaghetti under cold running water until cool. Drain.
- Add spaghetti, basil and parsley to vegetables and toss.
- Combine mayonnaise, garlic, vinegar and salt and pepper in small bowl.
- Add mayonnaise mixture to spaghetti mixture and toss well.
- Refrigerate until ready to serve. Serve cold or at room temperature.

Greek Chicken Salad

Contributed by Sharon Rolle

Yield: 6 servings

3 cups cubed cooked chicken

2 medium-sized cucumbers, peeled, seeded and chopped

10 ounces crumbled feta cheese

²/₃ cup sliced pitted black olives

¹/₄ cup snipped parsley

1 cup mayonnaise

2 cloves of garlic, crushed

¹/₂ cup plain yogurt

1 tablespoon ground or crushed oregano

- Mix chicken, cucumbers, feta cheese, olives and parsley in large bowl and set aside.
- Mix mayonnaise, garlic, yogurt and oregano in small bowl.
- Add mayonnaise mixture to chicken mixture.
- Toss lightly.
- Cover and chill.
- *Note:* Serve on bed of Boston lettuce or in pita bread pockets with romaine.

Smoked Turkey and Artichoke Salad

Contributed by Julie Lowe

Yield: 8 servings

3 pounds smoked turkey, cut into ¾-inch chunks

1 large red onion, cut into slivers

2   14-ounce cans artichoke hearts, quartered

2 celery stalks, thinly sliced

5 tablespoons lemon juice

7 tablespoons olive oil

1 teaspoon salt

1 teaspoon pepper

Dressing (recipe follows)

- Combine turkey, onion, artichoke hearts and celery in large bowl.
- Combine lemon juice, olive oil, salt and pepper, add to turkey mixture, and toss.
- Set aside at room temperature while preparing Dressing.
- Combine Dressing with turkey mixture and add salt and pepper to taste.
- Refrigerate for several hours to overnight.
- *Note:* Makes a great, unusual luncheon salad.

Dressing

2 egg yolks

1 whole egg

1½ tablespoons Dijon mustard

1½ tablespoons green peppercorns

2½ tablespoons tarragon

3 tablespoons lemon juice

1½ cups vegetable oil

1¼ cups olive oil

- Combine eggs, mustard, green peppercorns, tarragon and lemon juice in food processor and process for 20 seconds.
- Drizzle in vegetable oil and olive oil while machine is still running.

Shrimp Salad Mold

Contributed by Eleanor Thompson Pease

Yield: 6 servings

1 pound shrimp

2 envelopes unflavored gelatin

1/2 cup cold water

1/2 cup boiling water

2/3 cup mayonnaise

1/4 cup catsup

3 hard-boiled eggs, finely chopped

2 tablespoons capers

2 tablespoons lemon juice

1 tablespoon minced onion

Lettuce leaves

1 olive, sliced (for garnish)

- Cook, peel and devein shrimp.
- Chop shrimp finely.
- Soften gelatin in cold water.
- Add boiling water to gelatin and dissolve thoroughly. Let cool.
- Combine mayonnaise, catsup, eggs, capers, lemon juice and onion in large bowl.
- Add shrimp and gelatin. Blend well.
- Pour mixture into 4-cup fish-shaped mold or 6 individual molds and refrigerate for at least 4 hours or until set.
- Arrange lettuce leaves on platter or individual salad plates.
- Turn mold(s) out onto lettuce leaves and garnish with olive slices, using one slice to represent eye of fish for large fish mold.
- *Note:* Great as a luncheon salad or a festive addition to a buffet table.

Cream Cheese Pineapple Salad

Contributed by Mary Crowley   **Yield: 8 servings**

1 8-ounce can crushed pineapple, drained

1 cup sugar

1 tablespoon lemon juice or juice of 1 lemon

2½ tablespoons unflavored gelatin

¼ cup water

8 ounces cream cheese, softened

2 cups heavy cream

- Heat pineapple, sugar and lemon juice in saucepan.
- Mix gelatin and water in separate bowl.
- Add pineapple mixture to gelatin and cool slightly.
- Add cream cheese to pineapple mixture and beat with mixer.
- Beat heavy cream in separate bowl until thickened.
- Fold whipped cream into pineapple mixture.
- Pour mixture into serving dish and refrigerate until thickened.

Golden Fruit Medley

Contributed by Marge Grant   **Yield: 6 servings**

1 17-ounce can pear halves

1 3-ounce package peach gelatin

1 12-ounce can apricot nectar

1½ tablespoons lemon juice

Salt to taste

1 8-ounce can pineapple tidbits, drained

1 11-ounce can mandarin oranges, drained

- Drain pears and reserve ½ cup syrup.
- Bring pear syrup to a boil in large saucepan.
- Add gelatin to saucepan and stir until dissolved.
- Add nectar, lemon juice and salt.
- Chill mixture until consistency of egg whites.
- Fold drained fruit into gelatin mixture and pour into bowl or salad mold.
- Chill until set.

Garlic Dijon Salad Dressing

Contributed by Lynn Fuller

Yield: 1 cup

> 1/3 cup vinegar
> 1 clove of garlic, crushed
> 1/4 teaspoon salt
> 1/4 teaspoon pepper
> 1/4 teaspoon oregano
> 1 teaspoon Dijon mustard
> 2/3 cup olive oil

- Combine vinegar, seasonings and mustard in jar with tight-fitting lid and shake well.
- Add oil and shake vigorously.

Tangy Salad Dressing

Contributed by Kathy Altmaier

Yield: 10 servings

> 1/3 cup catsup
> 1 cup olive oil
> 1/4 cup white vinegar
> 1/2 cup sugar
> 1 tablespoon Worcestershire sauce
> 1 small red or white onion, finely chopped

- Blend all ingredients together in medium bowl with wire whisk.
- Refrigerate until ready to use.
- *Note:* This dressing goes very well with spinach salad.

Poppy Seed Salad Dressing

Contributed by Agnes Reilly

Yield: 12 servings

1½ cups sugar

2 teaspoons dry mustard

⅔ cup red or white wine vinegar

3 tablespoons onion juice

2 cups olive oil

2 tablespoons poppy seed

- Mix sugar, dry mustard and vinegar in bowl.
- Add onion juice and stir thoroughly.
- Add oil slowly, beating constantly until mixture is thickened.
- Add poppy seed and continue beating until blended thoroughly.
- Store dressing in refrigerator.

Herb Dressing

Contributed by Sunny McGeorge

Yield: 1 cup

¼ cup red wine vinegar

¼ cup apple cider vinegar

¼ cup safflower oil

⅓ cup olive oil

¾ teaspoon pepper

½ teaspoon garlic salt

¼ teaspoon dry mustard

¼ teaspoon turmeric

¼ teaspoon basil

Dash each of marjoram, thyme and rosemary

- Mix all ingredients in a large jar or container with tight lid.
- Refrigerate. Shake well before each use.

Aunt Jane's Cloud Biscuits

Contributed by Gail Nolen

Yield: 16 biscuits

2 cups sifted all-purpose flour

1 tablespoon sugar

4 teaspoons baking powder

½ teaspoon salt

½ cup shortening

1 egg, beaten

⅔ cup milk

- Preheat oven to 450 degrees.
- Sift flour, sugar, baking powder and salt into large bowl.
- Cut shortening into flour mixture with pastry blender until coarse crumbs form.
- Combine egg and milk and pour into flour mixture all at once. Stir until dough follows fork around bowl.
- Knead dough about 20 times on lightly-floured board.
- Roll out dough to ³/₄-inch thickness.
- Cut dough into rounds with 2-inch biscuit cutter. Do not twist biscuit cutter.
- Bake biscuits for 10 to 14 minutes.
- *Note:* These biscuits are light and airy. Unbaked biscuits can be chilled for 1 to 3 hours.

Brandywine Breakfast Cake

Contributed by Christine Johnson

Yield: 9 servings

2 cups all-purpose flour

1 cup sugar

5 tablespoons butter, softened

1 egg

3/4 cup buttermilk

1 teaspoon baking soda

1/4 cup plus 1 teaspoon packed brown sugar, divided

- Preheat oven to 350 degrees.
- Mix flour, sugar and butter in large bowl with pastry blender until crumbly.
- Reserve 2 tablespoons of flour mixture and set aside.
- Add egg, buttermilk, baking soda and 1/4 cup brown sugar to remaining mixture and blend well.
- Pour batter into greased 9-inch square baking pan.
- Combine reserved flour mixture and remaining brown sugar and sprinkle over batter.
- Bake for 20 to 30 minutes or until toothpick inserted near center comes out clean.
- *Note:* This cake freezes well. Thaw in refrigerator overnight for a morning treat.

Dill Bread

Contributed by Julie Lowe

Yield: 2 large loaves

½ cup warm milk, 105 to 115 degrees	¼ cup minced fresh or 2 tablespoons dried dill
3 tablespoons (4 envelopes) dry yeast	3 eggs, divided
4 teaspoons packed brown sugar	1 tablespoon salt
2 cups cottage cheese	½ teaspoon baking soda
¼ cup shortening	5 cups all-purpose flour
	1 tablespoon milk

- Combine warm milk, yeast and brown sugar in large bowl and whisk until blended. Let stand until foamy, about 10 minutes.
- Mix cottage cheese, shortening, dill, 2 eggs, salt and baking soda in food processor and process until smooth.
- Stir cottage cheese mixture into yeast mixture, blending well.
- Stir in flour 1 cup at a time, mixing thoroughly until dough comes away from side of bowl.
- Turn dough out onto lightly floured board and knead until smooth and elastic, about 10 minutes, adding more flour as needed.
- Clean bowl and grease generously. Transfer dough to greased bowl, turning to coat all sides.
- Cover bowl and let stand in warm place until dough is doubled in size, about 1¼ hours.
- Punch dough down and turn out onto lightly floured board.
- Knead in a little more flour if dough feels sticky. Divide dough into halves. Divide each dough half into thirds and roll into long strands.
- Braid 3 strands together to form loaf, tuck ends under and place on greased baking sheet. Repeat with remaining strands.
- Beat remaining egg and milk together to form egg wash.
- Brush loaves lightly with egg wash. Let loaves rise for 20 to 30 minutes.
- Preheat oven to 350 degrees. Bake loaves for 20 minutes.
- Brush with egg wash and bake for 5 minutes or until browned.
- Let loaves cool on wire rack.
- *Note:* Dough may also be shaped into loaves or individual rolls.

Easy Food Processor French Bread

Contributed by Julie Lowe   **Yield: 2 loaves**

3 cups bread or all-purpose flour, divided

1 teaspoon salt

1 tablespoon sugar

1 tablespoon butter

1 package (2½ teaspoons) active dry yeast

1 cup plus 2 tablespoons water at 120 to 130 degrees, divided

Cornmeal

1 tablespoon vegetable oil

1 egg white

1 tablespoon cold water

- Place 2 cups flour, salt, sugar, butter and yeast in bowl of food processor fitted with metal blade.
- Process until butter is thoroughly cut into dry ingredients.
- Add half of the hot water and pulse processor 4 times.
- Add remaining flour and hot water and pulse again 4 times.
- Let processor run until a ball of dough forms on the blade. If dough is too sticky, add more flour, 1 tablespoon at a time.
- When correct consistency is obtained, run processor for 40 to 60 seconds to knead dough.
- Turn out dough onto floured surface and knead several times to form smooth ball.
- Cover dough with plastic wrap and towel and let rest for 20 minutes.
- Divide dough in half and roll each piece out lightly to measure approximately 6x12 inches.
- Beginning at 12-inch side, roll each dough tightly, tapering ends by rolling back and forth.
- Grease baking sheet and sprinkle with a small amount of cornmeal.
- Place loaves on baking sheet.
- Brush loaves with vegetable oil, cover loosely with plastic wrap and refrigerate for 2 to 12 hours.
- Preheat oven to 425 degrees.
- Uncover loaves and let stand at room temperature for 10 minutes.
- Make several cuts on top of each loaf.
- Bake for 15 to 20 minutes.
- Brush loaves with egg white mixed with cold water and bake for 5 minutes longer or until golden brown.
- Cool on wire rack.

Granny's Best Cinnamon Buns

Contributed by Beth Ann Wahl   **Yield: 36 buns**

2 yeast cakes	1½ cups white raisins
1 cup sour cream	3 tablespoons cinnamon
3 eggs	1¾ cups packed brown sugar, divided
2½ cups butter, divided	
¼ cup sugar	¾ cup water
4 cups all-purpose flour	36 pecan halves
1 teaspoon salt	

- Let yeast, sour cream, eggs and butter stand until room temperature.
- Dissolve yeast in sour cream in measuring cup.
- Melt 1 cup butter and sugar together. Beat eggs with melted butter and sugar at low speed.
- Add sour cream mixture and beat at low speed.
- Sift flour 3 times. Combine with salt and add to mixer bowl 1 spoonful at a time, beating slowly until well mixed.
- Knead on floured surface for 5 minutes. Place dough in greased bowl and refrigerate, covered with towel, overnight.
- Roll dough into 3 less than ¼-inch thick squares on floured surface with floured rolling pin.
- Spread each with ¼ cup butter and sprinkle with ½ cup raisins, 1 tablespoon cinnamon and ⅓ cup brown sugar.
- Roll tightly as for jelly roll.
- Melt remaining butter.
- Place 1 teaspoon melted butter, 1 teaspoon water, 1 teaspoon brown sugar and 1 pecan half, top side down, in each of 36 muffin cups.
- Cut each roll into twelve ¾-inch thick slices and place slices cut side down in muffin cups.
- Let rise, covered, in warm place for 2 to 2½ hours.
- Preheat oven to 325 degrees.
- Bake for 10 minutes. Raise oven temperature to 350 degrees and bake for 10 minutes more. Raise oven temperature to 375 degrees and bake for 10 minutes more.
- *Note:* Can be frozen and reheated in microwave oven.

Cinnamon Bun Ring

Contributed by Pat Zolper

Yield: 12 servings

½ cup pecans

½ cup raisins

1   25-ounce package frozen dough balls

1   4-serving package vanilla pudding mix (not instant)

½ cup packed brown sugar

1 tablespoon cinnamon

½ cup butter

- Butter large tube pan.
- Cover bottom of pan with pecans and raisins, followed by frozen dough balls. Make sure bottom of pan is fully covered with dough balls.
- Combine pudding, sugar and cinnamon in separate bowl and sprinkle mixture over dough.
- Melt butter and pour over pudding layer.
- Let sit overnight or at least 10 hours, uncovered, at room temperature. Dough will more than triple in size.
- Line oven rack with foil to catch syrup bubbling over.
- Preheat oven to 350 degrees.
- Bake for 30 minutes.
- Let cool, then invert onto serving plate.

Clary Muffins

Contributed by Howard Anderson

Yield: 18 muffins

2¹/₂ cups oat bran

1¹/₂ cups whole wheat flour

1 tablespoon baking powder

1 teaspoon salt

1 teaspoon cinnamon

¹/₂ cup raisins

3 egg whites

1 large banana

¹/₃ cup maple syrup

¹/₃ cup honey

¹/₄ cup vegetable oil

1 teaspoon vanilla extract

1 cup skim milk

Chopped fresh fruit

Cranberry Butter (recipe on page 71)

- Preheat oven to 425 degrees.
- Combine oat bran, flour, baking powder, salt, cinnamon and raisins in large bowl and set aside.
- Combine egg whites, banana, maple syrup, honey, oil, vanilla and milk in blender. Add enough fresh fruit to bring mixture in blender to 4 to 4¹/₄ cups. Blend thoroughly.
- Pour blender mixture into flour mixture all at once and mix well. Add more milk if batter is not self-leveling.
- Pour batter into greased muffin cups and bake for 18 minutes.
- Let cool on wire rack.
- Serve with Cranberry Butter.
- *Note:* Chopped nuts may be substituted for all or part of the raisins. If this substitution is made, use almond extract in place of vanilla extract. White flour may also be substituted for part of the whole wheat flour, or more flour and less bran may be used for a lighter muffin. Try using apples, peaches, pears, plums, pumpkin, kiwi, guava, bananas, or even zucchini. Use your imagination to make these cholesterol lowering, appetite reducing, yummy muffins.

Cranberry Butter

Contributed by Karen Lazar

Yield: 1 cup

½ cup fresh cranberries

½ cup butter or margarine, cut into chunks

2 tablespoons confectioners' sugar

- Chop cranberries coarsely in food processor.
- Add butter and confectioners' sugar and process until well blended.

Blueberry Bread

Contributed by Becky Hamlin

Yield: 1 loaf

1¼ cups sugar, divided

1 egg

¼ cup shortening

½ cup milk

2⅓ cups all-purpose flour, divided

2 teaspoons baking powder

2 cups blueberries

¼ cup margarine, softened

½ teaspoon cinnamon

- Preheat oven to 375 degrees.
- Mix ¾ cup sugar, egg and shortening with electric mixer.
- Add milk then 2 cups flour and baking powder and mix well.
- Fold blueberries into batter.
- Spread batter in greased and floured loaf pan.
- Mix remaining sugar, remaining flour, margarine and cinnamon with fork to form topping.
- Sprinkle topping over batter.
- Bake for 45 to 50 minutes or until done.
- *Note:* Delicious and gooey.

Popovers

Contributed by Mary Rice

Yield: 6 large popovers

1 cup plus 2 tablespoons milk, at room temperature

1 tablespoon butter, melted

1 cup all-purpose flour

¼ teaspoon salt

2 eggs

- Preheat oven to 450 degrees.
- Whisk 1 cup milk into melted butter in large bowl with wire whisk.
- Add flour gradually, whisking until smooth.
- Add salt and stir to blend.
- Add eggs 1 at a time, whisking only until well blended. Do not overbeat.
- Add remaining milk, if needed, a little at a time until mixture coats spoon but is no thicker than heavy cream.
- Pour mixture into well greased popover pan or deep baking cups, filling cups no more than ²/₃ full.
- Place in oven immediately and bake for 15 minutes. Leave oven door closed.
- Reset oven to 350 degrees and bake for 20 minutes more. Do not open oven door during baking.
- Remove popovers from oven and serve immediately.
- *Note:* Popovers are delicious served with sweet butter and strawberry jam. A popover pan will produce beautifully browned, dramatically large popovers.

Apricot Nut Bread

Contributed by
Beverley Brainard Fleming

1½ cups dried apricots

½ cup butter

1 cup sugar

2 eggs, beaten

¾ cup orange juice

2 cups sifted all-purpose flour

1 tablespoon baking powder

¼ teaspoon baking soda

¾ teaspoon salt

1 teaspoon grated orange rind

1 cup chopped nuts

Yield: 10 servings

- Soak apricots in water for 30 minutes.
- Drain apricots, chop and set aside.
- Preheat oven to 350 degrees.
- Cream butter and sugar in large bowl.
- Add eggs and orange juice alternately to creamed mixture, beating thoroughly after each addition.
- Add flour, baking powder, baking soda, salt, orange rind, apricots and nuts and stir until well blended.
- Line 5x9-inch loaf pan with foil and butter foil.
- Pour mixture into prepared pan.
- Bake for 1½ hours.
- *Note:* This bread is delicious toasted, buttered and served with coffee.

Lemon Loaf

Contributed by
Beverley Brainard Fleming

½ cup shortening

1¼ cups sugar, divided

2 eggs

1½ cups all-purpose flour

½ teaspoon salt

1 teaspoon baking powder

Grated rind of 1 lemon

½ cup milk

Juice of 1 lemon, divided

Yield: 10 servings

- Preheat oven to 350 degrees.
- Cream shortening and 1 cup sugar in large bowl until light and fluffy.
- Add eggs 1 at a time to creamed mixture, beating until light and fluffy after each addition.
- Sift flour, salt and baking powder over creamed mixture.
- Sprinkle lemon rind over creamed mixture and stir to combine all ingredients.
- Add milk and ½ of the lemon juice and beat until well blended.
- Pour mixture into greased 5x9-inch loaf pan.
- Bake for 50 to 60 minutes or until top is golden brown.
- Remove loaf pan from oven.
- Combine remaining ¼ cup sugar and lemon juice in small bowl.
- Spread sugar mixture over hot loaf.
- Let loaf cool for 10 minutes and remove from pan.
- Let cool completely before slicing.
- *Note:* Delicious with afternoon tea.

Pumpkin Bread

Contributed by Beth Ann Wahl   **Yield: 10 servings**

1½ cups sugar

1⅔ cups all-purpose flour

1 teaspoon baking soda

¼ teaspoon baking powder

½ teaspoon nutmeg

¼ teaspoon ground cloves

½ teaspoon salt (optional)

1 cup canned pumpkin

½ cup vegetable oil

2 eggs or ½ cup egg substitute

- Preheat oven to 350 degrees.
- Combine all ingredients in large bowl and beat with large spoon.
- Pour mixture into greased 5x9-inch loaf pan or 2 small loaf pans.
- Bake for 1 hour or until loaves test done.
- *Note:* Doubles easily and freezes well, or store in refrigerator for up to a week.

Zucchini Bread

Contributed by Julie Lowe   **Yield: 2 loaves**

3 eggs, beaten

2 cups sugar

1 cup oil

2¼ cups all-purpose flour

2 teaspoons baking soda

1 teaspoon salt (optional)

½ teaspoon baking powder

1½ teaspoons cinnamon

¾ teaspoon nutmeg

¼ teaspoon allspice

2 cups shredded zucchini

1 cup chopped nuts

1 tablespoon vanilla extract

- Preheat oven to 350 degrees.
- Beat eggs with sugar and oil. Combine next 7 ingredients, add to egg mixture and stir. Mix in zucchini, nuts and vanilla.
- Pour mixture into 2 greased and floured large loaf pans.
- Bake for 1 hour and 10 minutes or until loaves test done.
- Cool in pans for 10 minutes, then remove from pans and cool on wire rack.

Soups ▪ Salads ▪ Breads

See also...

- Chilled Shrimp and Cucumber Soup
- Crab and Corn Bisque
- Lobster and Corn Chowder

...in the Restaurant Section

Meat and Poultry Entrees

Winterthur Museum and Gardens

For those who enjoy antiques, American decorative arts and colonial craftsmanship, a visit to Winterthur Museum and Gardens is in order. Here one can explore Henry Francis du Pont's vast collection of American furniture, painting, ceramics, and textiles. Universally acclaimed as the world's premier collection of American decorative arts, it is displayed in almost 200 rooms furnished in period style.

Steak Diane

Contributed by William Grabowski

Yield: 6 servings

6 sirloin steaks, 1/2-inch thick

Salt and pepper to taste

1/2 cup butter, divided

1/4 cup chopped scallions

1 teaspoon dry mustard

1 tablespoon Worcestershire sauce

1 cup sliced fresh mushrooms (optional)

2 tablespoons lemon juice

2 tablespoons chopped parsley

1 tablespoon chopped chives

Brandy to taste

- Trim fat from steaks and pound.
- Sprinkle steaks with salt and pepper.
- Melt 3 tablespoons butter in large skillet.
- Cook steaks in butter for 1 minute on each side. Remove steaks from skillet and set aside.
- Melt remaining butter in skillet, add scallions, mustard, Worcestershire sauce and mushrooms and cook until scallions are softened.
- Return steaks to skillet and cook for 1 minute more on each side.
- Add lemon juice, parsley and chives and heat through.
- Pour Brandy into spoon, ignite with match, and pour flaming Brandy over steaks.
- Cook for 1 to 2 minutes, then extinguish flames by covering with lid.
- Serve immediately.
- *Wine Suggestion:* French Red Burgundy

Beef Wellington

Contributed by Rosemarie Austin

Yield: 4 servings

¼ cup oil

1 clove of garlic

1   2 to 2½-pound filet
    tenderloin of beef

Pepper to taste

1 onion, finely chopped

1½ cups finely chopped
    mushrooms

3 tablespoons butter

2 tablespoons Cognac

1 tablespoon chopped herbs
    (thyme, parsley, etc...your
    choice)

1 sheet puff pastry

1 egg, beaten

- Preheat oven to 400 degrees.
- Heat oil in roasting pan in oven.
- Cut garlic clove in half, and rub over filet.
- Season filet with pepper.
- Roast filet for 20 to 25 minutes (rare).
- Set filet aside to cool.
- Sauté onion and mushrooms in butter for approximately 5 minutes or until soft.
- Add Cognac and herbs to onion and mushroom mixture, and let cool.
- Reset oven to 450 degrees.
- Roll pastry out on floured board to size that will completely cover filet.
- Lay cooled meat in center of pastry and spoon onion and mushroom mixture on top.
- Brush pastry edges with water, fold pastry over filet carefully, and seal.
- Brush pastry surface with egg.
- Bake for 20 to 30 minutes or until pastry is browned.
- Slice and serve immediately.
- *Wine Suggestion:*
  French Bordeaux, such as St. Estephe

Festive Beef Tenderloin

Contributed by Kathy Benson

Yield: 12 servings

1 cup catsup

1 teaspoon Worcestershire sauce

2 1-ounce envelopes dry Italian dressing mix

2 teaspoons Dijon mustard

1½ cups water

1 4 to 6-pound beef tenderloin, trimmed

■ Combine all ingredients except tenderloin and mix well to make marinade.

■ Spear tenderloin in several places and place in heavy plastic bag or pan.

■ Pour marinade over tenderloin and seal tightly.

■ Refrigerate for at least 8 hours, turning occasionally.

■ Drain tenderloin and reserve marinade.

■ Preheat oven to 425 degrees.

■ Place tenderloin on rack in baking pan and insert meat thermometer.

■ Bake for 30 to 45 minutes, basting occasionally with marinade, until meat thermometer reads 140 degrees for rare or 150 degrees for medium rare.

■ Remove tenderloin to serving platter and let rest for 10 minutes before carving.

■ Heat remaining marinade and serve over tenderloin.

■ *Wine Suggestion:* California Zinfandel

Filet de Boeuf au Poivre

Contributed by Joan Gehrke

Yield: 6 servings

1 whole beef tenderloin, approximately 4 pounds

¼ cup Brandy

1 tablespoon fresh coarsely ground black pepper

1 green onion, finely minced

2 cloves of garlic, finely minced

Salt to taste

- Tie tail of beef under to make roast approximately same thickness for whole length.
- Combine Brandy, pepper, onion and garlic in small bowl. Rub into roast, sprinkle with salt and let stand for at least 1 hour.
- Preheat oven to 400 degrees.
- Roast beef for 35 to 45 minutes or until meat thermometer reads 130 degrees for rare.
- Remove from oven. Let rest for 15 to 20 minutes before carving.
- *Wine Suggestion:* Châteauneuf-du-Pape

Beef with Dill Marinade

Contributed by Michelle Wright

Yield: 4 servings

⅔ cup olive oil

3 tablespoons white wine vinegar

3 tablespoons dry Sherry

2 tablespoons fresh lemon juice

¾ teaspoon dry mustard

½ teaspoon pepper

1½ tablespoons minced fresh dill

1½ pounds lean beef, cut into 1-inch cubes

- Mix all ingredients except beef cubes. Pour over beef cubes and chill, covered, for at least 8 hours.
- Drain beef cubes and place loosely on skewers.
- Grill or broil to desired doneness, turning to brown all sides.
- *Note:* Also good as a marinade for vegetables, especially mushrooms or vegetable kabobs using mushrooms, onions, peppers or cherry tomatoes.
- *Wine Suggestion:* Zinfandel

Easy Eye-of-Round

Contributed by Michelle Wright

1 eye-of-round roast
1 tablespoon olive oil
1 tablespoon lemon pepper
1 tablespoon garlic powder

Yield: ¹/₂ pound per person

- Preheat oven to 500 degrees.
- Rub roast lightly with olive oil, then sprinkle evenly with lemon pepper and garlic powder.
- Bake in shallow pan for 4 to 5 minutes per pound.
- Turn off oven, but do not open door.
- Leave roast in oven according to weight:
  1¹/₄ hours if less than 2 pounds,
  1¹/₂ hours if 2 to 3 pounds, or
  2 hours if 3 to 4 pounds. Roast will be medium rare.
- *Wine Suggestion:*
  California Merlot

Jan's Burgundy Roast

Contributed by Kathy Segars

1 eye-of-round roast

1   10-ounce can golden mushroom soup

1/2 soup can Burgundy wine

Yield: 4 ounces per serving

- Preheat oven to 500 degrees.
- Place roast in shallow roasting pan and bake for 4 to 5 minutes per pound.
- Turn off oven. Leave roast in closed oven for 1¼ hours plus an additional 15 minutes for each pound over 2 pounds.
- Slice roast very thinly and place slices in chafing dish. Combine soup and wine, pour over meat and heat well.
- *Note:* Serve with small rolls.
- *Wine Suggestion:* California Cabernet Sauvignon

Barbecued Beef

Contributed by Betty Reilly

3 to 4 pounds chuck roast, English cut, or London broil

1 medium-sized onion, chopped

1 teaspoon celery salt

1 teaspoon Worcestershire sauce

1/2 teaspoon Tabasco sauce

1/3 cup packed brown sugar

1/2 teaspoon garlic juice

1 tablespoon chili powder

1/2 cup water

Yield: 8 servings

- Place beef in roasting pan or slow-cooker.
- Combine all remaining ingredients and pour over beef.
- Preheat oven to 350 degrees if using oven.
- Bake, covered, until meat pulls apart easily, approximately 3 to 4 hours in oven or according to instructions on slow-cooker.
- *Beverage Suggestion:* Red Zinfandel or a lager beer

Beef Burgundy

Contributed by Angela B. Case

Yield: 6 servings

3 pounds beef cubes

1/4 cup shortening

3 tablespoons all-purpose flour

1 1/2 teaspoons salt

1/2 teaspoon pepper

1 teaspoon thyme

1 cup beef broth

1 cup dry red wine

1 3-ounce can mushrooms or 1/2 pound fresh mushrooms, sliced

12 small white pearl onions

- Preheat oven to 325 degrees.
- Brown beef in shortening in large skillet.
- Stir in flour and seasonings.
- Turn into 3-quart casserole dish.
- Stir in broth and wine.
- Cover and bake for 2 hours.
- Add mushrooms and onions.
- Bake for 1 hour more.
- Add more wine and broth if additional liquid is needed.
- *Note:* Serve over rice or noodles.
- *Wine Suggestion:* Red Côtes du Rhone

Felicia's Famous Stroganoff

Contributed by Kearsley Walsh

Yield: 6 servings

1 1/2 pounds London broil

1 10-ounce can cream of mushroom soup

1 1-ounce package dry onion soup mix

2 cups sour cream

1 8-ounce package egg noodles, cooked

- Preheat oven to 350 degrees.
- Cut London broil into slices and place in bowl. Add mushroom soup and onion soup mix. Mix thoroughly.
- Bake, covered, in 9x13-inch casserole dish for 45 minutes.
- Uncover and bake for 15 minutes more or to desired doneness.
- Add sour cream and mix well.
- Pour meat mixture over noodles.
- Serve immediately.

Beef Stew

Contributed by Margaret Bartoli

Yield: 6 servings

1 to 1½ pounds beef cubes

Flour for dredging

1 tablespoon olive oil

1 beef bouillon cube

⅝ cup warm water

8 ounces vegetables, canned or fresh

3 to 4 potatoes, diced

1 cup water

½ tablespoon packed brown sugar

2 tablespoons tapioca

2 tablespoons bread crumbs

1 bay leaf

¼ cup wine

- Preheat oven to 250 degrees.
- Dredge beef cubes lightly in flour.
- Brown beef cubes in oil in large skillet.
- Place browned beef cubes in 2-quart casserole dish.
- Dissolve bouillon cube in warm water.
- Add dissolved bouillon, vegetables and 1 cup water to casserole dish.
- Sprinkle remaining ingredients over top.
- Bake, covered, for 6 to 7 hours, adding water as necessary if stew becomes too thick.
- Discard bay leaf.
- *Wine Suggestion:* Zinfandel

Classic Stroganoff

Contributed by Susan Kremer

Yield: 4 servings

1 pound sirloin steak

2 tablespoons butter or margarine

½ pound mushrooms, sliced

½ cup minced onion

1   10-ounce can beef consommé

2 tablespoons catsup

1 small clove of garlic, minced

1 teaspoon salt

Pepper to taste

3 tablespoons all-purpose flour

1 cup sour cream

1   8-ounce package egg noodles

- Cut steak into thin slices.
- Melt butter in skillet, add mushrooms and onion, and sauté until tender.
- Remove mushrooms and onion from pan.
- Add sliced steak to same skillet and brown lightly on both sides.
- Set aside half of consommé.
- Add remaining consommé, catsup, garlic, salt and pepper to steak in pan.
- Cover and simmer for 15 minutes.
- Add reserved consommé and flour to pan, blending thoroughly.
- Add mushroom and onion mixture.
- Heat to boiling, stirring constantly. Boil for 1 minute.
- Add sour cream. Heat through, but do not boil.
- Prepare noodles according to package instructions.
- Serve stroganoff over hot noodles.
- *Wine Suggestion:* California Cabernet Sauvignon

Pepper Steak

Contributed by Ellen Douglas

Yield: 4 servings

2 pounds strip steak, cut into strips

1 tablespoon paprika

3 tablespoons margarine, divided

1 beef bouillon cube

1 cup hot water

1 to 2 red bell peppers

2 to 3 green bell peppers

1 medium-sized onion

2 tablespoons cornstarch

¼ cup soy sauce

- Cover beef strips with paprika.
- Melt 1 tablespoon margarine in large skillet.
- Add meat and brown.
- Dissolve bouillon in hot water and add to skillet.
- Simmer over low heat for 30 minutes.
- Slice peppers and onion into thin rings.
- Sauté vegetables in remaining margarine in separate skillet until onion is lightly golden.
- Add cornstarch to meat mixture skillet. Cook until thickened, stirring constantly, then stir in soy sauce.
- Add sautéed vegetables to meat mixture skillet and stir to combine.
- *Note:* Serve over rice or noodles.
- *Wine Suggestion:* Chilean Cabernet Sauvignon

Sweet and Sour Meatballs

Contributed by Sandy Pembleton

Yield: 6 servings

1 pound ground beef

1 egg, beaten

1 cup bread crumbs

2 tablespoons chopped onion

2 tablespoons milk

3/4 teaspoon salt

1 8-ounce can pineapple
   tidbits

1 8-ounce can cranberry
   sauce

1/2 cup barbecue sauce

1/4 teaspoon salt

Pepper to taste

1 tablespoon cornstarch

1/4 cup cold water

1/2 cup green bell pepper strips

- Combine first 6 ingredients and shape into approximately twenty-four 1-inch meatballs.
- Brown meatballs in skillet and drain.
- Drain pineapple and reserve liquid in measuring cup. Set aside pineapple.
- Add water to reserved pineapple liquid to make 3/4 cup.
- Mix liquid with cranberry and barbecue sauce, salt and pepper.
- Pour mixture over meatballs in skillet and bring to a boil. Reduce heat and simmer for 15 to 20 minutes.
- Combine cornstarch and cold water and add to skillet.
- Stir well and cook until thick and bubbly, stirring constantly.
- Add pineapple and pepper strips and cook until heated through.
- Serve over rice.
- *Wine Suggestion:* California Zinfandel

Beef Moussaka

Contributed by Julie Lowe   **Yield: 6 servings**

1 pound ground beef	2 eggs, separated
3 medium onions, chopped	1/2 cup bread crumbs
1 tablespoon chopped parsley	2 tablespoons butter
1/3 cup water	2 tablespoons all-purpose flour
1 tablespoon tomato paste	1 cup milk
2 teaspoons salt	Salt and pepper to taste
1/2 teaspoon pepper	1 cup grated Parmesan cheese
1 large or 2 medium eggplant	

- Preheat oven to 350 degrees.
- Brown meat in heavy skillet.
- Add onions, parsley, water, tomato paste, salt and pepper and mix. Cover and simmer for 25 minutes, stirring occasionally.
- Grease baking sheets lightly with vegetable oil.
- Slice eggplant into 1/4-inch thick slices, lay on baking sheets and bake for 12 to 15 minutes or until lightly browned.
- Beat egg whites until foamy.
- Add egg whites to meat mixture, then add bread crumbs and stir until absorbed.
- Layer 1/3 of the eggplant slices, half the meat mixture, half the remaining eggplant slices, remaining meat mixture and remaining eggplant in 2-quart casserole dish.

- Melt 2 tablespoons butter in medium saucepan. Add flour and cook for 1 minute.
- Add milk to saucepan, stirring until smooth to make cream sauce. Cook over medium heat until thickened.
- Beat egg yolks slightly and slowly drizzle into cream sauce, stirring constantly.
- Season cream sauce with salt and pepper to taste.
- Pour cream sauce over top of casserole and top with cheese.
- Bake, covered, for 30 minutes or until bubbly and lightly browned.
- *Note:* Ground lamb may be substituted for ground beef. Recipe may be prepared ahead and refrigerated or frozen prior to baking.
- *Wine Suggestion:* Spanish Rioja

Genoese Meatballs

Contributed by Jane Martin

1 pound ground veal

3 tablespoons bread crumbs

1 clove of garlic, crushed

$^1/_3$ cup finely chopped fresh parsley or other fresh herbs

$^1/_3$ cup chopped fresh mushrooms

2 tablespoons grated Parmesan cheese

1 egg, lightly beaten

$^1/_2$ teaspoon nutmeg

Salt and pepper to taste

Yield: 6 servings

- Combine all ingredients in large bowl and mix well.
- Shape mixture into small oval meatballs.
- Broil meatballs for 10 to 15 minutes on one side or until brown, turn meatballs over, and broil for 5 minutes more or until brown.
- *Note:* May be served alone or with tomato or cream sauce.
- *Wine Suggestion:* California Merlot

Pot o' Beans

Contributed by Michelle Wright

8 ounces bacon

1 pound lean ground beef

$^1/_2$ cup chopped onion

1   16-ounce can pork and beans

1   15-ounce can each kidney beans and butter beans

1   16-ounce can white beans

1 cup catsup

$^1/_2$ cup packed brown sugar

1 tablespoon dry mustard

1 tablespoon vinegar

Yield: 12 servings

- Preheat oven to 350 degrees.
- Brown bacon, ground beef and onion, and drain well.
- Combine bacon, ground beef and onion mixture with remaining ingredients in 3-quart casserole dish.
- Bake, covered, for 2 hours.
- *Note:* Can also be prepared in slow-cooker.
- *Beverage Suggestion:* Yuengling Lager

Veal Chops with Cognac Cream

Contributed by Cyndy Brown

Yield: 2 servings

2 1½ to 2-inch thick veal
   chops

2 tablespoons butter

1 shallot, minced

Salt and pepper to taste

⅓ cup white wine

¼ cup heavy cream

1 teaspoon Cognac

- Remove chops from refrigerator ½ hour before preparing.
- Melt butter in nonstick skillet.
- Brown chops on medium-high heat, for approximately 3 minutes per side.
- Add shallot to skillet and season with salt and pepper.
- Cover skillet, lower heat and cook for 10 minutes.
- Turn chops over, add white wine, cover skillet and cook for 8 minutes more.
- Remove chops to warmed plates.
- Add cream and Cognac to skillet, bring to slow boil and cook until thickened, stirring constantly.
- Pour sauce over chops and serve.
- *Wine Suggestion:* French Pouilly Fuissé

Oriental Lamb Chops

Contributed by a Friend

Yield: 6 servings

12 lamb chops
Salt and pepper to taste
3 tablespoons olive oil
2 tablespoons Dijon mustard
2 tablespoons dry white wine
1/2 cup mango chutney, puréed
2/3 cup peanuts, chopped

- Preheat oven to 400 degrees.
- Sprinkle chops with salt and pepper.
- Sauté chops in oil over high heat until golden brown and rare inside.
- Transfer chops to well greased baking dish.
- Mix mustard and wine until smooth.
- Brush mustard mixture on chops and sprinkle with chutney and peanuts.
- Bake chops for 5 minutes.
- *Note:* Cherry tomatoes make a colorful garnish for this unusual dish.
- *Wine Suggestion:* Australian Shiraz

Aunt Lynne's Lemon Glazed Pork Loin

Contributed by Karen Lazar

Yield: 4 servings

1   1½-pound boneless pork loin

1 tablespoon olive oil

Salt and pepper to taste

⅔ cup sugar

⅔ cup lemon juice

2 shallots, chopped

¼ cup Brandy

- Preheat oven to 400 degrees.
- Rub pork loin with just enough olive oil to coat, then rub with salt and pepper.
- Place pork loin in roasting pan and cook for 25 minutes.
- Combine remaining ingredients in stainless steel or enamel saucepan and boil until glaze turns amber color and becomes syrupy.
- Brush pork loin with all of the glaze.
- Cook for 15 additional minutes.
- Remove pork loin from oven and let stand for 15 minutes.
- Slice pork loin thinly and arrange on serving platter.
- Drizzle with glaze from roasting pan.
- *Wine Suggestion:* French Sancerre or Beaujolais

Spiced Spareribs Singapore

Contributed by Connie Greendoner

Yield: 6 servings

4 cloves of garlic

1½ teaspoons salt

½ teaspoon pepper

½ teaspoon Five Spice powder

1 tablespoon honey

1 tablespoon sesame oil

3 tablespoons soy sauce

3 pounds country-style pork spareribs

½ cup hot water

- Preheat oven to 350 degrees.
- Crush garlic with salt.
- Add pepper, Five Spice powder, honey, sesame oil and soy sauce to garlic mixture.
- Rub seasoning mixture into ribs.
- Roast ribs for 30 minutes.
- Turn ribs over, add hot water to pan, and roast ribs for 35 minutes more or to desired doneness, basting every 10 minutes.
- *Note:* This spicy dish may also be prepared by either frying the ribs in oil until brown, adding water, and simmering, covered, for 30 minutes, or grilling the ribs for about 25 minutes, turning once.
- *Beverage Suggestion:* Sapporo Draft Beer

Chicken Barbecue Sauce

Contributed by Marnie Rodgers

Yield: 2 cups

¹/₂ cup each cider vinegar and white vinegar

²/₃ cup vegetable oil

2 teaspoons Worcestershire sauce

1 clove of garlic, diced

1 large onion, sliced

1¹/₂ teaspoons salt

¹/₂ teaspoon paprika

3 tablespoons catsup

¹/₂ teaspoon dry mustard

Tabasco sauce to taste

- Combine all ingredients in blender and mix well.
- Refrigerate.
- *Note:* Use for grilling or baking chicken or spareribs. Can be stored in refrigerator for several weeks.

Mustard-Sauced Chicken

Contributed by Linda Miller

Yield: 6 servings

3 whole chicken breasts, skinned, boned and halved

2 tablespoons butter or margarine

1 clove of garlic, minced

¹/₂ teaspoon rosemary

¹/₃ cup white wine

1 tablespoon Dijon mustard

Pepper to taste

- Preheat oven to 350 degrees.
- Wash chicken and pat dry. Place chicken in ovenproof 9x13-inch glass baking dish.
- Melt butter in skillet. Add garlic and rosemary to skillet and sauté for 2 minutes.
- Add wine and boil for 2 minutes.
- Remove from heat and blend in mustard. Brush on chicken and sprinkle with pepper.
- Bake for 35 minutes, basting with mustard sauce every 10 minutes.

Capacola Chicken

Contributed by Stephanie Fortunato

Yield: 8 servings

4 whole chicken breasts, skinned, boned and halved

8 slices Cheddar, Swiss or Monterey Jack cheese

Dijon or honey mustard to taste

Tarragon to taste

Pepper to taste

16 slices hot and spicy capacola ham

2 eggs, slightly beaten

²/₃ cup Italian-style bread crumbs

2 tablespoons margarine or butter

¼ cup white wine

- Preheat oven to 350 degrees.
- Wash chicken and pat dry.
- Top each chicken breast with a slice of cheese, then top with mustard, tarragon and pepper.
- Wrap each chicken breast in 2 slices of ham.
- Dip wrapped chicken breasts in eggs.
- Place wrapped chicken breasts side by side in 9x13-inch casserole dish lightly greased with nonstick cooking spray.
- Sprinkle bread crumbs on top and dab with margarine.
- Pour wine into casserole dish, but not on top of chicken.
- Bake, uncovered, for 1 hour.
- Serve immediately.
- *Wine Suggestion:*
  Australian Shiraz or
  Australian Semillon/Chardonnay

Chinese Smoked Chicken

Contributed by Connie Greendoner

Yield: 4 servings

1   3 to 4-pound whole chicken fryer

1 green onion, chopped

6 tablespoons soy sauce

2 tablespoons hoisin sauce

2 tablespoons dry white wine

1 tablespoon packed brown sugar

1 teaspoon finely minced ginger

1 teaspoon salt

1 teaspoon liquid smoke

- Wash chicken and pat dry. Tie wings close to chicken.
- Combine remaining ingredients in bowl and mix well to make marinade.
- Place chicken and marinade in cooking bag. Tie bag closed and rotate so marinade coats chicken. Refrigerate overnight.
- Preheat oven to 350 degrees.
- Remove chicken from refrigerator. Cut slits in bag. Place bag in 9x13-inch pan.
- Bake for 90 minutes.
- Cool slightly before serving.
- *Note:* Chicken parts can be substituted for whole chicken, or use marinade with chicken wings as an appetizer.
- *Wine Suggestion:* California Zinfandel or French Pouilly Fumé

Chicken Monterey

Contributed by Cathy duPont Schlaeppi   **Yield: 6 servings**

4 whole chicken breasts, skinned, boned and halved

Salt to taste

Black pepper to taste

Paprika to taste

1/2 cup plus 2 tablespoons all-purpose flour, divided

1/2 cup butter or margarine, divided

1/2 cup chopped onion

1/2 pound mushrooms, sliced

1 clove of garlic, minced

1/2 teaspoon celery salt

1/2 teaspoon white pepper

1 cup chicken broth

1/2 cup white wine

1/4 teaspoon white wine Worcestershire sauce

1 1/2 cups shredded Monterey Jack cheese, divided

- Preheat oven to 350 degrees.
- Wash chicken breasts and pat dry.
- Place chicken breasts between 2 sheets of waxed paper and pound to 1/4-inch thickness.
- Combine salt, black pepper, paprika and 1/2 cup flour in small paper bag.
- Add 1 chicken breast at a time to bag and shake until well coated.
- Melt 1/4 cup butter in large skillet and sauté chicken until golden brown. Remove chicken from skillet and place in 3-quart shallow baking dish.
- Melt remaining butter in skillet and sauté onion, mushrooms and garlic until tender, but not brown.
- Add remaining flour, celery salt, white pepper, chicken broth, wine and Worcestershire sauce to skillet, stir and cook over low heat until mixture is thickened.
- Add 1/2 cup cheese to mixture and blend well.
- Pour mixture over chicken breasts, top with remaining cheese and sprinkle with paprika.
- Bake for 20 to 30 minutes or until cheese melts.
- *Note:* May be prepared a day ahead and baked just before serving.
- *Wine Suggestion:* California Pinot Noir or Italian Pinot Grigio

Curried Chicken

Contributed by Mary Rice

Yield: 8 servings

½ cup butter or margarine, melted

½ cup honey

2 tablespoons Dijon mustard

1 tablespoon curry powder

4 whole chicken breasts, skinned, boned and halved

- Preheat oven to 325 degrees.
- Mix butter, honey, mustard and curry powder in bowl.
- Wash chicken and pat dry. Place in buttered 9x13-inch casserole dish. Pour honey mixture over chicken, turning chicken to coat.
- Bake, uncovered, for 40 minutes, basting occasionally with honey mixture.
- *Note:* Serve with rice.
- *Wine Suggestion:* California Gewurztraminer

Honey Mustard Chicken

Contributed by Diane Bold

Yield: 6 servings

2 tablespoons sesame seeds

3 tablespoons honey

¼ cup Dijon mustard

¼ cup Sherry or white wine

1 tablespoon lemon juice

3 whole chicken breasts, skinned, boned and halved

- Preheat oven to 400 degrees.
- Toast sesame seeds in small skillet over medium heat for approximately 5 minutes or until golden brown.
- Remove sesame seeds from heat and add honey, mustard, wine and lemon juice. Mix well.
- Wash chicken and pat dry. Arrange in 9x13-inch baking dish. Pour mixture over chicken.
- Bake, uncovered, for 50 minutes, basting occasionally.
- *Note:* This dish freezes well.
- *Wine Suggestion:* French Vouvray

Glazed Chicken Cordon Bleu

Contributed by a Friend

Yield: 8 servings

1 tablespoon vegetable oil

1 small onion, chopped

2 teaspoons curry powder

2 teaspoons dry mustard

½ cup prune juice

⅓ cup apricot jam

¼ cup red wine vinegar

2 tablespoons cornstarch

2 tablespoons water

4 whole chicken breasts, skinned, boned and halved

8 slices prosciutto ham

8 slices Swiss cheese

- Preheat oven to 350 degrees.
- Heat oil on low in small saucepan.
- Add onion and curry powder, and cook for 5 minutes, stirring frequently.
- Add mustard, prune juice, apricot jam and vinegar.
- Bring mixture to a boil, stirring constantly until jam melts, approximately 1 minute.
- Mix cornstarch and water in small bowl, and add to saucepan, stirring constantly until mixture is clear and thickened, approximately 3 to 4 minutes. Set aside.
- Wash chicken and pat dry.
- Lay chicken flat in shallow 9x13-inch casserole dish or baking pan.
- Place 1 slice ham and 1 slice cheese on each half chicken breast.
- Roll up each breast with ham and cheese inside and secure with toothpick.
- Brush with glaze.
- Bake for 25 to 30 minutes, basting occasionally with glaze.
- Remove chicken from oven and brush with remaining glaze.
- *Wine Suggestion:* Alsacian Gewurztraminer

Moo Goo Gai Pan

Contributed by Donna Kelloway

Yield: 4 servings

1 pound chicken breast meat, cut into bite-sized pieces

1 egg white

1 teaspoon wine

1 tablespoon plus 2 teaspoons cornstarch, divided

4 tablespoons oil, divided

3 slices gingerroot

6 ounces snow peas

4 ounces mushrooms, sliced

1/4 teaspoon garlic salt

3/4 cup chicken broth

1 tablespoon water

- Wash chicken and pat dry.
- Combine egg white and wine in large bowl.
- Add chicken to bowl and toss.
- Sprinkle 2 teaspoons cornstarch over chicken and toss again. Set aside to marinate.
- Heat 3 tablespoons oil in large wok or skillet, add gingerroot, and cook for a few seconds.
- Add chicken to wok and stir-fry over high heat until chicken is white. Remove chicken from wok and set aside.
- Heat remaining oil in wok, add snow peas, mushrooms and garlic salt and stir.
- Reduce heat to medium, add chicken broth, and bring to a boil.
- Add chicken mixture to wok and heat until boiling.
- Combine remaining cornstarch and water and add to chicken mixture. Mix well and heat until thickened, stirring constantly.
- Serve immediately.
- *Note:* Broccoli or asparagus may be substituted for snow peas.
- *Wine Suggestion:* California Sparkling wine or German Riesling

Nichols Chicken

Contributed by Jane Mullen

Yield: 4 servings

2 whole chicken breasts, skinned, boned and halved

1 8-ounce can sauerkraut, drained

4 slices Swiss cheese

1 cup Thousand Island dressing

- Preheat oven to 350 degrees.
- Place chicken in casserole dish and top with drained sauerkraut and cheese slices.
- Cover chicken with dressing.
- Bake for 1 hour.
- *Wine Suggestion:* German Riesling

Party Chicken

Contributed by Anne Noble

Yield: 6 servings

3 whole chicken breasts, skinned, boned and halved

1 tablespoon oil

1 1/2-ounce package dry Italian dressing mix

8 ounces cream cheese, softened

1 10-ounce can mushroom soup

1/4 cup white wine

1/2 cup sliced fresh mushrooms

- Preheat oven to 325 degrees.
- Wash chicken and pat dry.
- Brown chicken in skillet in oil and Italian dressing mix.
- Place chicken in ungreased 9x13-inch baking dish.
- Combine cream cheese, mushroom soup and wine, and pour over chicken.
- Bake for 50 minutes.
- Add mushrooms and bake for 10 minutes more.
- *Wine Suggestion:* Chardonnay

Steph's Chicken

Contributed by Stephanie Grant

Yield: 4 servings

¼ cup butter or margarine

2 tablespoons mustard

¼ cup all-purpose flour

⅓ cup seasoned bread crumbs
  or stuffing mix

1 teaspoon chopped parsley

2 teaspoons seasoning mix

¼ teaspoon pepper

2 whole chicken breasts,
  skinned, boned and halved

¼ cup grated Cheddar cheese

- Preheat oven to 350 degrees.
- Melt butter and stir in mustard. Set aside.
- Combine flour, crumbs, parsley and seasonings.
- Wash chicken and pat dry.
- Dredge each chicken piece in butter mixture, then flour mixture, and then place in glass baking dish.
- Bake for 35 minutes.
- Top chicken with cheese and bake for 10 minutes more.
- *Wine Suggestion:*
  California Chenin Blanc

Sweet and Tangy Cranberry Chicken

Contributed by Sandy Pembleton

Yield: 6 servings

8 ounces Sweet and Tangy French dressing

1   10-ounce can whole berry cranberry sauce

1/2   1-ounce package dry onion soup mix

2 to 3 pounds chicken parts

- Preheat oven to 300 degrees.
- Combine French dressing, cranberry sauce and onion soup mix.
- Wash chicken and pat dry.
- Place chicken in 9x13-inch baking dish.
- Pour cranberry mixture over chicken.
- Bake for 90 minutes.
- *Note:* Chicken breasts, skinned, boned and halved, may be substituted for chicken parts. Reduce baking time to 1 hour if this substitution is made. Delicious served over rice.
- *Wine Suggestion:* California Gewurztraminer

Cornish Game Hens in Creamy Tarragon Sauce

Contributed by Beth Ann Wahl   **Yield: 4 servings**

4 Rock Cornish game hens, about 3/4 pound each	3 tablespoons finely chopped shallots
Salt to taste	1/3 cup dry white wine
Freshly ground pepper to taste	1/2 cup half and half
1 1/4 teaspoons tarragon, divided	1 tablespoon finely chopped parsley
2 tablespoons butter or margarine	

- Preheat oven to 450 degrees.
- Wash hens inside and out and pat dry.
- Sprinkle hens inside and out with salt and pepper.
- Place 1/4 teaspoon tarragon in cavity of each hen.
- Truss hens.
- Melt butter on stove top in shallow roasting pan large enough to hold hens.
- Place hens, breast side up, in pan and brush with butter.
- Transfer hens to oven when butter starts to sizzle.
- Bake for 15 minutes.
- Baste hens and continue baking for 20 minutes more, basting occasionally.
- Remove hens from oven, transfer to serving platter and cover with foil to keep warm.

- Spoon off fat from roasting pan and discard.
- Add shallots and cook on stove top until soft.
- Add wine and cook, stirring to deglaze roasting pan, about 30 seconds.
- Add any juices accumulating on hen platter to roasting pan and stir.
- Simmer until liquid is reduced by half, then add half and half and remaining tarragon.
- Strain sauce and pour over hens.
- Sprinkle with parsley.
- *Note:* If larger hens are used, total oven cooking time should be increased to approximately 50 to 60 minutes.
- *Wine Suggestion:* Full-bodied California Chardonnay

Teriyaki Duck

Contributed by Chuck Wright

Yield: 4 servings

½ teaspoon garlic powder

¼ teaspoon ground red pepper

¼ teaspoon lemon pepper

2 whole large partially frozen
   wild duck breasts, skinned,
   boned and halved

1 cup teriyaki sauce

- Combine garlic powder, red pepper and lemon pepper.
- Slice frozen duck into ½-inch slices as you would slice London broil.
- Sprinkle seasoning mixture on duck slices.
- Place duck slices in flat pan or casserole dish and cover with teriyaki sauce.
- Refrigerate for 4 to 6 hours.
- Grill duck slices for 8 minutes or until medium rare, turning once.
- *Wine Suggestion:* Washington State Merlot

Breast of Duck a la Zinfandel

Contributed by a Friend

Yield: 8 servings

3 shallots, chopped

2 tablespoons margarine

1½ cups Zinfandel wine

2 tablespoons plum jam

2 cups chicken broth

Salt and pepper to taste

4 whole duck breasts, skinned, boned and halved

3 tablespoons olive oil

1   16-ounce can peaches, drained

- Preheat oven to 375 degrees.
- Sauté shallots in margarine in large skillet until tender.
- Add wine and jam to skillet and simmer for 20 minutes.
- Add broth to skillet and simmer for 10 to 15 minutes more to make sauce.
- Season sauce with salt and pepper and keep warm.
- Brown duck breasts in oil in separate skillet.
- Transfer duck breasts to 9x13-inch baking dish and bake for 7 to 8 minutes. Drain duck breasts on paper towels.
- Divide sauce evenly among 8 plates and top with duck breasts. Garnish with peaches and serve immediately.
- *Wine Suggestion:* California Zinfandel

Poultry Entrees

Turkey-Stuffed Peppers

Contributed by Nancy Higgins

Yield: 2 servings

2 medium-sized green bell
  peppers

1/2 pound ground turkey

3/4 cup chopped onion

1 clove of garlic, minced

1 tablespoon margarine

1 tablespoon all-purpose flour

1/2 cup skim milk

1/2 cup chopped unpeeled
  tomato

1/4 cup shredded sharp
  Cheddar cheese, divided

White pepper to taste

2 teaspoons reduced-calorie
  mayonnaise

- Preheat oven to 350 degrees.
- Cut off tops of peppers and remove seed and membrane.
- Boil peppers until soft, approximately 4 minutes. Drain and set aside.
- Brown turkey, onion and garlic in skillet coated with nonstick cooking spray. Drain.
- Melt margarine in saucepan, add flour and cook for 1 minute, stirring constantly.
- Add milk to saucepan gradually, and cook until thick and bubbly, stirring constantly.
- Combine turkey mixture, white sauce, tomato, half the cheese, white pepper and mayonnaise in large bowl. Mix well.
- Spoon mixture into peppers and top with remaining cheese.
- Place peppers in 8x10-inch baking dish and bake for 15 minutes.
- Broil 8 inches from the broiler for 3 to 5 minutes to melt cheese.
- Serve immediately.
- *Note:* Serve with brown rice for a healthy, low-calorie meal.
- *Wine Suggestion:* Chardonnay

Meat and Poultry Entrees

See also...

- Brandywine Duck for Two
- Chicken Diablo
- Chicken Pomodoro
- Chicken Salad with Basil-Lime Vinaigrette
- Costolette di Agnello alla Griglia (Grilled Rack of Lamb)
- Dijon-Hoisin Crusted Pork Tenderloin with Three Pepper Marmalade
- Rack of Lamb with Mustard-Peppercorn Crust
- Roast Pheasant
- Stuffed Quail
- Veal Marengo

...in the Restaurant Section

Fish and Shellfish Entrees

Walker's Mill

Colonial millers found the Brandywine River to be a dependable source of power. Industry prospered throughout the eighteenth and nineteenth century. The first millers exported flour around the world. Mills producing cotton and paper soon flourished along the Brandywine's regal banks, such as Walker's Mill pictured here.

Creamy Flounder Parmesan

Contributed by Mary Rice

Yield: 4 servings

2 pounds fresh flounder filets

Flour for dredging

1/2 cup unsalted butter, divided

1 cup sour cream

1/4 cup fresh coarsely grated
  Parmesan cheese

1/2 cup seasoned bread crumbs

- Preheat oven to 350 degrees.
- Dredge filets in flour lightly.
- Melt 2 tablespoons butter in large skillet and sauté filets a few at a time until golden brown on both sides, adding more butter as needed. Set aside.
- Combine sour cream and cheese.
- Place half the filets in a casserole dish and top with half the sour cream mixture. Repeat.
- Melt remaining butter in skillet where fish was cooked, scraping brown bits from pan into melting butter.
- Add bread crumbs to skillet and cook until brown, stirring constantly.
- Pour crumb mixture over final sour cream layer.
- Heat for 20 minutes just prior to serving.
- *Note:* Purchase a chunk of Parmesan cheese and grate it coarsely just before use to add a special freshness to this dish.
- *Wine Suggestion:* French Meursault

Penne, Peppers and Salmon in Garlic Sauce

Contributed by Jane Martin

Yield: 4 servings

½ cup heavy cream

4 cloves of garlic, lightly crushed

¼ cup fresh lemon juice

¾ cup olive oil

2 tablespoons minced fresh dill

2 tablespoons minced fresh parsley

Salt and pepper to taste

1 pound penne or other tubular pasta

6 ounces thinly sliced smoked salmon, cut into ⅓-inch x 2-inch strips

1 large red bell pepper, cut into fine julienne strips

1 large green bell pepper, cut into fine julienne strips

1 small red onion, thinly sliced

4 dill sprigs

- Bring cream to a boil in saucepan over moderate heat.
- Add garlic and simmer for 15 minutes or until garlic is softened and cream is reduced to about ¼ cup.
- Purée mixture in food processor or blender until very smooth. Add lemon juice and blend well.
- Add oil in slow stream with motor running, blending until emulsified.
- Blend in dill, parsley, salt and pepper. Set sauce aside.
- Cook penne in large pot of boiling salted water until tender. Drain and transfer to large bowl.
- Set aside 16 smoked salmon strips for garnish.
- Toss penne, peppers, onion and remaining smoked salmon gently.
- Add sauce and toss gently.
- Divide mixture among 4 plates and garnish each serving with 4 strips of reserved salmon and dill sprig.
- Serve warm or at room temperature.
- *Note:* A delightful luncheon dish. Half portions can be served as appetizers.
- *Wine Suggestion:* Oregon Pinot Noir

Poached Salmon with Mustard-Caper Sauce

Contributed by Tracey Mulvaney   **Yield: 4 servings**

4 salmon steaks	2 teaspoons cornstarch
4 lemon slices	2 tablespoons water
1 cup chicken broth	1 egg yolk, beaten
1/4 cup white wine	2 teaspoons capers
White pepper to taste	1 teaspoon Dijon mustard

- Place salmon in lightly greased skillet.
- Place a lemon slice on top of each salmon steak.
- Combine chicken broth, wine and pepper.
- Pour broth mixture over salmon.
- Cover and simmer for 10 minutes or until salmon flakes easily.
- Remove lemon slices and salmon from skillet. Set aside and keep warm.
- Boil broth mixture gently for 5 minutes or until reduced to approximately 1/4 cup.
- Dissolve cornstarch in water and stir into reduced broth.
- Continue to cook, stirring constantly, until mixture is thick and bubbly.
- Cook 1 additional minute, stirring constantly.
- Whisk half the broth mixture into egg yolk gradually, using wire whisk. Return mixture to skillet.
- Cook for 2 minutes.
- Stir in capers and mustard.
- Place salmon on platter and cover with sauce.
- Serve immediately.
- *Wine Suggestion:*
  French Beaujolais or
  White Bordeaux such as Graves

Baked Shad and Roe

Contributed by
Senator William V. Roth, Jr.

Yield: 3 servings

1 medium to large shad, split

1 set shad roe

1 cup sour cream

Paprika to taste

4 lemon slices

- Preheat oven to 400 degrees.
- Place shad skin side down in shallow baking dish.
- Lay a piece of roe on each piece of shad. Cover with thick layer of sour cream.
- Sprinkle with paprika.
- Top each piece of shad with 2 thin lemon slices.
- Bake for 30 minutes.
- *Wine Suggestion:* California Pinot Noir or French White Burgundy

Salmon Steaks with Creamy Tomato Sauce

Contributed by Cam Martin

Yield: 4 servings

1 fish bouillon cube

2 cups clam juice or 2 cups water

½ cup chopped celery

½ cup chopped carrots

1 cup white wine

1 cup heavy cream

2 tablespoons tomato paste

Tabasco sauce to taste

4 salmon steaks

- Dissolve bouillon cube in clam juice or water. Combine with celery, carrots and wine in large saucepan and boil for 15 minutes.
- Combine cream, tomato paste and Tabasco sauce in heavy skillet and boil until thickened and slightly reduced, stirring constantly. Keep warm.
- Strain bouillon mixture into fish poacher, add salmon and poach until salmon flakes easily. Place salmon on serving platter.
- Pour warm cream mixture over poached salmon.

Shad with Fresh Bread Crumbs

Contributed by Beth Ann Wahl

Yield: 4 servings

9 slices white or whole wheat
 bread

Seasoning mix to taste

Fresh tarragon to taste

1½ cups margarine, melted

3 large fresh shad filets

1 lemon, cut into wedges

- Preheat oven to 450 degrees.
- Place bread slices in blender or food processor and grind to fine crumbs.
- Place crumbs in large bowl, add seasoning mix, tarragon and margarine and mix well.
- Place shad filets on 9x13-inch broiler pan.
- Bake for 15 minutes. Do not broil.
- Remove pan from oven and cover filets with bread crumb mixture.
- Reset oven to 350 degrees.
- Bake for 12 minutes more.
- Serve immediately with lemon wedges.
- *Wine Suggestion:* French Muscadet

Marinated Swordfish

Contributed by Bettie Reilly

Yield: 4 servings

2 tablespoons soy sauce

2 tablespoons orange juice

1 tablespoon olive oil

1 tablespoon catsup

1 tablespoon chopped parsley

1 small garlic clove, minced

1/2 teaspoon lemon juice

1/4 teaspoon pepper

1/4 teaspoon oregano

4 swordfish steaks

- Combine all ingredients except swordfish in small bowl to make marinade.
- Place fish in glass pan and cover with marinade.
- Marinate for 1 to 3 hours at room temperature, basting frequently.
- Preheat oven to 350 degrees.
- Bake swordfish for 30 minutes, or until fish flakes easily.
- *Wine Suggestion:* California Fumé Blanc

Broiled Fish with Garlic and Tarragon

Contributed by Joan Gehrke

Yield: 4 servings

1/4 cup mayonnaise

1 to 2 cloves of garlic, minced

1 teaspoon tarragon

1 pound fresh mild fish filets

- Combine mayonnaise, garlic and tarragon in small bowl.
- Spread mixture on filets.
- Broil approximately 2 inches from heat source for 5 to 12 minutes or until filets flake easily.
- *Note:* This recipe works well with both flounder and monkfish. May also be prepared on an outdoor grill. To do so, place fish on heavily-oiled foil and cook 4 to 6 inches above a medium flame.
- *Wine Suggestion:* Italian Pinot Grigio

Sautéed Trout with Grapes and Almonds

Contributed by a Friend

Yield: 2 servings

1 cup all-purpose flour

Salt and pepper to taste

12 ounces trout, boned and butterflied

½ cup half and half

¼ cup olive oil

6 tablespoons butter or margarine

⅓ cup lemon juice

1 cup fresh white grapes

½ cup sliced almonds

- Combine flour with salt and pepper.
- Dip trout in half and half and dredge with seasoned flour.
- Sauté trout in oil in skillet for approximately 5 to 6 minutes or until golden brown on both sides.
- Drain trout on paper towels.
- Sauté butter until lightly browned.
- Stir in lemon juice, grapes and almonds.
- Place trout on warm plates and pour mixture over trout.
- *Note:* Garnish with lemon wedges and parsley.
- *Wine Suggestion:* California White Burgundy

Shrimp Casserole

Contributed by Karen Lazar

Yield: 4 servings

1   14-ounce can artichoke hearts

1 pound medium shrimp, cooked, peeled and deveined

1/4 pound fresh mushrooms, sliced

6 1/2 tablespoons butter, divided

4 1/2 tablespoons all-purpose flour

1 1/2 cups half and half

1 tablespoon Worcestershire sauce

1/4 cup dry Sherry

Salt and pepper to taste

1/4 cup grated Parmesan cheese

Paprika to taste

Chopped parsley to taste

- Preheat oven to 375 degrees.
- Drain artichokes, quarter and arrange in 1-quart casserole dish.
- Place shrimp over artichokes.
- Sauté sliced mushrooms in 2 tablespoons butter for 6 minutes.
- Spoon mushrooms over shrimp.
- Melt remaining butter over low heat in saucepan, add flour and stir for 3 to 5 minutes.
- Stir in half and half slowly, and cook until thickened to make cream sauce, stirring constantly.
- Add Worcestershire sauce, Sherry, salt and pepper to cream sauce.
- Pour cream sauce over contents of casserole dish.
- Sprinkle cheese on top and dust with paprika.
- Bake for 20 minutes.
- Sprinkle with parsley before serving.
- *Wine Suggestion:* California Chardonnay

Jambalaya

Contributed by Anne Taylor

Yield: 6 servings

3 tablespoons shortening

2 tablespoons all-purpose flour

1 cup chopped onion

½ cup chopped celery

1 clove of garlic

1   28-ounce can tomatoes, chopped

1 tablespoon basil

1 bay leaf

Salt to taste

1 cup uncooked rice

1 pound raw shrimp, peeled

1½ cups water

Cayenne pepper to taste

- Heat shortening in large pot.
- Stir in flour and cook over low heat, stirring frequently, until golden brown to make roux.
- Add onion, celery and garlic to roux and cook over low heat until onion is translucent.
- Add tomatoes, basil, bay leaf and salt and cook, covered, over low heat for 25 minutes.
- Add rice, shrimp, water and cayenne pepper and cook, covered, over low heat for 30 minutes or until rice is tender, adding more water if mixture appears dry.
- Discard bay leaf.
- *Note:* Up to 1 pound diced, cooked chicken and/or kielbasa sausage may be added, if desired.
- *Beverage Suggestion:* Dos Equis Beer

Shrimp in Sour Cream Sauce

Contributed by Linda Miller

Yield: 4 servings

¼ cup butter or margarine

½ pound fresh mushrooms, sliced

2 cloves of garlic, diced

1 tablespoon chopped fresh basil

1 pound (16 to 20) shrimp, shelled and deveined

1 cup sour cream

Pepper to taste

- Melt butter in large skillet.
- Add mushrooms, garlic and basil to skillet, and sauté until soft.
- Add shrimp to skillet, and sauté until pink and plump.
- Stir in sour cream and pepper.
- *Note:* Serve over rice, noodles or in individual casserole dishes.
- *Wine Suggestion:* A regional Chardonnay

Crab Cakes

Contributed by Cathy Scanlon

Yield: 6 crab cakes

1 pound lump crab meat

2 eggs

3 tablespoons light cream

1 onion, minced

1 scallion, minced

¼ teaspoon cayenne pepper

¼ teaspoon Dijon mustard

Pepper to taste

Cracker crumbs

2 tablespoons vegetable oil

- Mix crab meat, eggs, cream, onion, scallion, cayenne pepper, mustard and pepper in large bowl.
- Add cracker crumbs until mixture can be formed into cakes.
- Form into 6 cakes and coat each cake lightly with cracker crumbs.
- Fry cakes in oil in large skillet for approximately 5 minutes on each side or until lightly browned.
- *Wine Suggestion:* Italian Gavi

Crab Imperial

Contributed by Mr. Henry E. I. duPont

Yield: 6 servings

2 tablespoons butter

2 tablespoons all-purpose flour

1 cup heavy cream

1 cup mayonnaise

1 egg, beaten

1/2 cup dry Sherry

1/2 teaspoon salt

White pepper to taste

2 cups mashed potatoes

1 pound jumbo lump crab meat

Paprika to taste

- Preheat oven to 350 degrees.
- Melt butter in saucepan, stir in flour, then add cream and cook until thickened, stirring constantly. Set aside to cool.
- Combine cooled cream mixture, mayonnaise, egg, Sherry, salt and pepper to make sauce.
- Place mashed potatoes in pastry bag and pipe around edges of casserole dish.
- Place crab meat in center of casserole dish and cover with sauce.
- Sprinkle with paprika.
- Bake for 30 to 40 minutes or until hot and bubbly.
- Serve immediately.
- *Note:* May also be prepared in individual serving dishes to make an elegant presentation.
- *Wine Suggestion:* California or Washington State Johannisberg Riesling

Hot Crab Casserole

Contributed by Donna Everson

Yield: 8 servings

1 large green bell pepper, chopped

1 small onion, chopped

1 cup chopped celery

1 pound crab meat

1 cup mayonnaise

¼ teaspoon salt

¼ teaspoon pepper

1 teaspoon Worcestershire sauce

1 cup bread crumbs

2 tablespoons butter, melted

- Preheat oven to 350 degrees.
- Mix green pepper, onion, celery and crab meat.
- Mix in mayonnaise, salt, pepper and Worcestershire sauce.
- Turn mixture into lightly greased 3-quart casserole dish.
- Combine bread crumbs with butter and sprinkle over casserole.
- Bake for approximately 30 minutes or until bubbly.
- *Note:* Shrimp may be substituted for crab meat.
- *Wine Suggestion:* Sauvignon Blanc/Semillon Blend

Scallops Florentine

Contributed by Karen Lazar

Yield: 8 servings

4 10-ounce packages frozen chopped spinach, cooked

½ cup margarine, divided

Nutmeg to taste

Salt and pepper to taste

2½ pounds large scallops, quartered

¼ cup chopped shallots

½ cup white wine

¼ cup all-purpose flour

1 cup heavy cream

Parmesan cheese to taste

- Preheat oven to 450 degrees.
- Squeeze excess moisture from spinach.
- Toss spinach with 2 tablespoons margarine, nutmeg, salt and pepper.
- Place spinach mixture in greased 9x13-inch baking dish and set aside.
- Melt 2 tablespoons margarine in large saucepan. Add scallops, salt, pepper, shallots and wine, and bring to a boil.
- Remove saucepan from heat and transfer scallops to bowl. Reserve liquid from saucepan in separate bowl.
- Melt remaining margarine in saucepan. Add flour. Cook until mixture is bubbly, stirring constantly.
- Add reserved liquid and cream to flour mixture and cook over medium heat until thickened to make sauce, stirring constantly. Remove from heat.
- Place scallops over spinach mixture and top with sauce. Sprinkle with Parmesan cheese.
- Bake for 5 minutes, then broil for 5 to 7 minutes or until browned.
- *Wine Suggestion:* White Bordeaux

Shrimp and Scallops in Pastry Shells

Contributed by Jane Martin

Yield: 8 servings

¼ cup unsalted butter, divided

1½ pounds medium shrimp, shelled and deveined

1½ pounds bay scallops, rinsed

½ cup heavy cream

⅛ teaspoon arrowroot

2 tablespoons minced fresh or 2 teaspoons dried tarragon

Fresh lemon juice to taste

Cayenne pepper to taste

Salt to taste

8 frozen pastry shells

8 tarragon leaves for garnish

- Heat 2 tablespoons butter in large skillet over moderately high heat until hot.
- Sauté shrimp for 3 minutes.
- Transfer shrimp with slotted spoon to separate bowl.
- Heat remaining butter in skillet, and sauté scallops for 1 minute.
- Transfer scallops with slotted spoon to bowl with shrimp.
- Cook pan juices over medium-high heat for 1 minute.
- Add juices that have accumulated in shellfish bowl, cream and arrowroot to skillet, and simmer for 3 minutes or until slightly thickened, stirring constantly.
- Stir in minced tarragon, lemon juice, cayenne pepper and salt. Add shrimp and scallops.
- Cook over medium heat until shellfish are heated through. Keep warm.
- Prepare pastry shells according to package instructions.
- Top pastry shells with shellfish mixture and garnish with tarragon leaves.
- *Wine Suggestion:* Australian Chardonnay

Curried Seafood Casserole

Contributed by Mary Ball Morton

Yield: 8 servings

4 shallots, chopped

1 tablespoon curry powder

3 tablespoons butter or margarine

3 tablespoons all-purpose flour

1 cup chicken broth, heated

2 cups half and half

Freshly ground pepper to taste

1 pound raw shrimp, peeled, deveined and sliced lengthwise

1 pound back-fin crab meat

- Preheat oven to 325 degrees.
- Sauté shallots and curry powder in butter.
- Blend in flour.
- Add chicken broth, half and half and pepper, stirring until smooth.
- Mix in seafood, and cook for 2 minutes.
- Place mixture in buttered 2-quart casserole dish and bake for 45 minutes.
- *Wine Suggestion:* California Fumé Blanc

Seafood Scampi

Contributed by Helen deLeon

Yield: 4 servings

1 pound large shrimp, peeled and deveined

1 pound scallops

2 tablespoons olive oil

1 tablespoon minced garlic

1/2 teaspoon lemon rind or red pepper flakes (optional)

1/4 cup dry white wine

1/4 cup butter, cut into pieces

2 green onions, sliced

- Cook shrimp and scallops in oil in large skillet for 3 to 7 minutes depending on size or until done. Remove from skillet; keep warm.
- Add garlic and lemon rind to skillet, and cook for 30 seconds.
- Add wine to skillet and cook until reduced by half.
- Remove skillet from heat and whisk in butter, 1 piece at a time.
- Return shrimp and scallops to skillet, add green onions and toss to coat.

Fish and Shellfish Entrees

See also...

- Baked Salmon Filets Briabe
- Bay Scallops Gruyère
- Broiled Catfish with Asparagus and Thyme-Tomato Vinaigrette
- Flounder Français with Lemon-Garlic Cream Sauce

...in the Restaurant Section

Pasta · Eggs · Cheeses

Hagley Museum

Step into America's industrial past at the Hagley Museum. This 240-acre site along the banks of the Brandywine River brings together the best of American industrial history with some of the most stunning views of the rocky river nestled among enormous stately trees. Here you can visit Eleutherian Mills, the delightful 1803 home of Eleuthere Irenee du Pont as well as the first office of the Du Pont Company, and twenty-three of the original stone gunpowder mills, one of which is pictured here. Children particularly enjoy the many working models and demonstrations.

Chicken-Pecan Fettucini

Contributed by Betty Reilly

Yield: 4 servings

¾ cup butter, divided

1 pound skinned and boned chicken breasts, cut into ¾-inch pieces

3 cups sliced mushrooms

1 cup sliced green onions

½ teaspoon salt, divided

½ teaspoon pepper, divided

½ teaspoon garlic powder, divided

10 ounces fettucini

1 egg yolk

⅔ cup half and half, room temperature

2 tablespoons chopped fresh parsley

½ cup grated Parmesan cheese

1 cup pecans, toasted and chopped

- Melt ¼ cup butter in skillet.
- Wash chicken and pat dry.
- Add chicken to skillet and sauté until lightly browned.
- Remove chicken from skillet and set aside.
- Sauté mushrooms and green onions in skillet drippings.
- Return chicken to skillet and simmer until done, approximately 15 minutes. Add ¼ teaspoon salt, ¼ teaspoon pepper and ¼ teaspoon garlic powder and set aside.
- Cook fettucini according to package instructions and drain.
- Melt remaining butter and combine with egg yolk, half and half, parsley and remaining salt, pepper and garlic powder.
- Stir mixture into hot fettucini.
- Add Parmesan cheese and chicken mixture and toss.
- Sprinkle with pecans.
- *Wine Suggestion:* California Chardonnay

Alice's Seafood Primavera

Contributed by Alice Kelly

Yield: 4 servings

3 tablespoons butter or margarine

3 tablespoons all-purpose flour

1 cup milk, half and half or evaporated skim milk

1 tablespoon Sherry

Pepper to taste

1 hard-boiled egg, chopped

1 cup cooked seafood (shrimp, scallops, crab, lobster, "sea legs," in any combination)

1 cup fresh or frozen broccoli, cooked and cut into bite-sized pieces

1/2 cup fresh or frozen carrots, cooked and sliced

1/2 cup fresh or frozen peas, cooked

1/2 cup sliced mushrooms, freshly cooked or canned

8 ounces angel hair pasta or thin spaghetti

- Melt butter in saucepan and add flour to make roux.
- Whisk in milk slowly. Cook until thickened, stirring constantly.
- Add Sherry and pepper.
- Toss together egg, seafood and vegetables, add mixture to saucepan and stir.
- Cook pasta according to package instructions and drain.
- Serve seafood mixture over pasta.
- *Wine Suggestion:* Chilean Chardonnay

Capellini Primavera

Contributed by B. Gary Scott   **Yield: 6 servings**

1 tablespoon olive oil

1/2 medium-sized onion, coarsely chopped

3 large tomatoes, peeled, seeded and chopped

1 cup chicken broth

1/2 cup heavy cream or evaporated skim milk

1 pound broccoli flowerets, coarsely chopped

1 large carrot, julienned

1 pound capellini

2 medium-sized zucchini, julienned

1 1/2 cups freshly grated Parmesan cheese

1/4 cup unsalted butter

Salt and pepper to taste

- Bring large pot of salted water to a boil over high heat.
- Heat olive oil in large skillet over medium heat.
- Add onion to skillet, and cook until translucent, for about 5 minutes.
- Add tomatoes to skillet, and cook for 1 to 2 minutes, stirring constantly.
- Mix broth and cream into tomato mixture to make sauce. Remove sauce from heat and keep warm.
- Add broccoli to boiling water and cook until water returns to a boil.
- Stir carrot and capellini into boiling water, heat until water boils again, and boil for 3 minutes.
- Add zucchini to pot and cook until capellini is *al dente*, about 2 to 3 minutes more.
- Drain capellini mixture and transfer to large bowl.
- Add cheese and butter to capellini mixture and toss until butter is melted.
- Pour sauce over capellini mixture and toss gently.
- Season with salt and pepper and serve immediately.
- *Note:* Vegetables may be cut in advance and covered with damp paper towels until ready for use.
- *Wine Suggestion:* Merlot

Linguine with Herbs

Contributed by Sheila DiSabatino

Yield: 4 servings

1 9-ounce package fresh linguine

2 tablespoons olive oil

1 small red onion, chopped

1 cup low-fat milk

3/4 cup grated Parmesan cheese

3 thin slices prosciutto ham, cut into 3-inch strips

1 teaspoon basil

1 teaspoon parsley

1 teaspoon mint

Salt and pepper to taste

- Cook linguine *al dente* according to package instructions and drain.
- Heat olive oil in pot large enough to hold entire recipe, including linguine.
- Cook onion in oil until soft.
- Add milk, cheese, ham, basil, parsley, mint, salt and pepper.
- Heat through and keep sauce warm.
- Add pasta to sauce and toss.
- Heat again and serve hot on warm platter.
- *Wine Suggestion:* Italian Soave

Captain's Linguine

Contributed by Marc Wilson

Yield: 6 servings

¼ cup olive oil

16 large shrimp

½ pound sea or bay scallops

4 ounces garlic, chopped
(approximately 2 heads)

1 teaspoon basil

½ teaspoon chili powder

3 green bell peppers, julienned

1 large red onion, julienned

¾ cup diced tomatoes

¼ cup Brandy

¼ cup dry white wine

¼ pound jumbo lump crab
meat

½ pound linguine, cooked
according to package
instructions and drained

Grated Parmesan cheese to
taste

Chopped fresh parsley to taste

- Heat olive oil in large skillet.
- Add shrimp and scallops to oil
  and cook until opaque.
- Add garlic, basil and chili
  powder and cook for 1 minute.
- Add peppers, onion, tomatoes,
  Brandy, wine and crab meat.
- Cook until vegetables are tender.
- Place hot linguine in large
  serving dish.
- Pour mixture over linguine and
  garnish with Parmesan cheese
  and parsley.
- *Note:* Yes, the amount of garlic is
  correct. This is a delicious,
  garlicky dish.
- *Wine Suggestion:* French Chablis

Spaghetti Carbonara

Contributed by Hazel Kirk

Yield: 6 servings

1 pound spaghetti

½ pound bacon, cut into ¼-inch pieces

½ cup heavy cream

¼ teaspoon red pepper flakes

Freshly ground black pepper to taste

3 eggs

⅔ cup Parmesan cheese

¼ cup butter, softened

- Begin cooking spaghetti according to package instructions.
- Fry bacon until crisp while spaghetti is cooking.
- Pour off all but 2 tablespoons of fat from bacon.
- Add cream, red pepper flakes and pepper to bacon and simmer gently to keep warm while spaghetti is cooking.
- Beat eggs in small bowl. Add Parmesan cheese to eggs.
- Drain spaghetti and toss with butter and egg-cheese mixture. The heat of the pasta will cook the eggs.
- Add bacon-cream mixture and toss.
- Serve immediately.
- *Wine Suggestion:* Italian Barbaresco

Pesto Tortellini

Contributed by Janice Watson

1   12-ounce package cheese tortellini

1 cup Pesto Sauce (recipe follows)

1 tomato, peeled, seeded and chopped

1 zucchini, chopped

2 green onions, chopped

1   4-ounce package mozzarella string cheese, chopped

3 tablespoons pine nuts

4 ounces black olives, halved

Salt and pepper to taste

Yield: 3 servings as a main dish or 6 servings as a side dish

- Cook tortellini according to package instructions and drain.
- Toss all ingredients together.
- Serve warm or chilled.
- *Wine Suggestion:* Sauvignon Blanc

Pesto Sauce

2 to 3 cups fresh basil leaves

½ cup olive oil

2 tablespoons pine nuts

2 to 3 cloves of garlic, minced

½ cup grated Parmesan cheese

2 tablespoons grated Romano cheese

3 tablespoons butter, softened

Yield: 1 cup

- Blend basil, olive oil, pine nuts and garlic in food processor.
- Pour into bowl and blend in cheeses and butter by hand.

Pesto with Cream Cheese

Contributed by Theresa Capuano

Yield: 10 servings

1 cup loosely packed fresh
  basil leaves
  (approximately 1 ounce)

8 ounces cream cheese

1 tablespoon finely chopped
  parsley

1 tablespoon finely chopped
  fresh mint

1/2 cup olive oil

3/4 cup freshly grated
  Parmesan cheese

Salt to taste

Freshly ground black pepper
  to taste

1 1/2 pounds spaghetti or other
  pasta

- Place basil, cream cheese, parsley and mint in food processor.
- Blend thoroughly, gradually adding oil.
- Add cheese, salt and pepper and continue blending until mixed thoroughly.
- Cook spaghetti according to package instructions and drain.
- Serve basil mixture over hot pasta.

Pasta with Fresh Tomato Sauce

Contributed by Linda Miller

Yield: 4 servings

3 large tomatoes

1/2 cup olive oil

3 cloves of garlic, minced

1 teaspoon basil

Salt and pepper to taste

8 to 12 ounces pasta

Grated Parmesan cheese to taste

- Peel tomatoes, chop and place in bowl.
- Add olive oil, garlic, basil, salt and pepper and mix well.
- Let sit for at least 2 hours.
- Cook pasta according to package instructions and drain.
- Mix together pasta and tomato sauce.
- Add cheese and serve immediately.
- *Wine Suggestion:* California or Italian Merlot

Oriental Linguine

Contributed by Linda Shaffer

Yield: 4 servings

1 pound fresh or 12 ounces dried linguine

1/4 cup oriental sesame oil

3 tablespoons soy sauce

1/4 teaspoon freshly ground black pepper

1/4 cup chopped watercress leaves

1/4 cup finely chopped red bell pepper

1 small clove of garlic, minced

- Cook linguine according to package instructions and drain.
- Combine sesame oil, soy sauce and pepper in large bowl.
- Add linguine to oil mixture and toss.
- Add watercress, bell pepper and garlic and toss until mixed.
- Serve at room temperature.
- *Note:* This dish may be prepared the day before serving.

Tri-Color Veggie Pasta

Contributed by Becky Hammell

Yield: 8 servings

1 medium-sized onion, thinly sliced

1 tablespoon olive oil

1 clove of garlic, slivered

2 small yellow bell peppers, thinly sliced

2 small red bell peppers, thinly sliced

2 small zucchini, julienned

2 small yellow squash, julienned

Salt and pepper to taste

8 ounces tube-shaped pasta (Mostaccioli)

3 tablespoons unsalted butter

3 tablespoons all-purpose flour

1½ teaspoons rosemary

½ teaspoon sage

1 bay leaf

1½ cups milk

1½ cups grated Fontina or mozzarella cheese

- Preheat oven to 425 degrees.
- Cook onions in oil in large skillet until translucent.
- Add garlic and peppers to skillet and cook for 5 minutes, stirring frequently.
- Add zucchini and yellow squash and cook for 5 minutes more, stirring frequently. Season with salt and pepper and remove from heat.
- Cook pasta according to package instructions and drain.
- Melt butter in large saucepan and add flour, rosemary, sage and bay leaf. Cook for 2 minutes, stirring constantly.
- Add milk to saucepan slowly, stirring constantly with wire whisk. Cook until mixture is consistency of heavy cream, stirring constantly. Remove from heat.
- Combine pasta, milk mixture, vegetables and 1 cup cheese and pour into buttered 3-quart baking dish.
- Top with remaining cheese, and bake for 20 to 30 minutes or until top is crusty and brown.

Oriental Shrimp and Pasta Salad

Contributed by Mary McBrier

Yield: 6 servings

12 ounces fettucini

1/2 cup white wine vinegar

6 tablespoons lemon juice

3 tablespoons honey

3 tablespoons finely chopped fresh ginger

2 cloves of garlic, finely chopped

2 tablespoons soy sauce

Cayenne pepper to taste

1 1/2 pounds shrimp, shelled and deveined

2 tablespoons sesame oil

1 cup chopped green onions

1 to 2 tablespoons grated lemon peel

Chopped walnuts (optional)

- Cook fettucini according to package instructions and drain. Let cool.
- Mix vinegar, lemon juice, honey, ginger, garlic, soy sauce and cayenne pepper in large saucepan.
- Bring mixture to a boil.
- Cook shrimp in vinegar mixture in small batches for approximately 1 minute.
- Set shrimp aside and reserve vinegar mixture.
- Combine pasta, shrimp, vinegar mixture, sesame oil, green onions, lemon peel and walnuts.
- Toss well and refrigerate overnight.
- Serve cold.

Crab Meat Pasta Salad

Contributed by Cabby Flynn

Yield: 6 servings

1 pound spaghetti

5 hard-boiled eggs, chopped

5 stalks celery, chopped

6 sweet pickles, chopped

1/4 small onion, finely chopped

1/2 pound crab meat

1 1/2 cups mayonnaise

Salt and pepper to taste

Parmesan cheese to taste

- Cook spaghetti according to package instructions and drain. Let cool.
- Combine all remaining ingredients except cheese and mix well.
- Pour mixture over spaghetti and toss well.
- Sprinkle with Parmesan cheese.

Felicia's Baked Ziti

Contributed by Kearsley Walsh

Yield: 10 servings

1 pound ziti

1 pound Italian sausage, crumbled

1/2 pound ground beef, crumbled

1 cup chopped onion

1 cup chopped green bell pepper

2   8-ounce cans tomato sauce

4 ounces grated Parmesan cheese, divided

1/4 cup each fresh basil and oregano leaves, chopped

12 ounces grated mozzarella cheese

- Preheat oven to 350 degrees.
- Cook ziti according to package instructions and drain.
- Brown sausage and ground beef with onion and green pepper in large skillet. Drain fat.
- Add tomato sauce, half the Parmesan cheese, basil and oregano to sausage mixture.
- Toss mixture with cooked ziti and place in 9x13-inch casserole dish.
- Sprinkle with mozzarella and remaining Parmesan cheese.
- Bake, uncovered, for 20 minutes.
- *Wine Suggestion:* Italian Chianti

Turkey and Ziti Casserole

Contributed by Governor and
Mrs. Thomas R. Carper

8 ounces ziti

1　30-ounce jar spaghetti
　sauce

1½ cups cubed turkey or
　3　5-ounce cans turkey

8 ounces shredded mozzarella
　cheese, divided

1 tablespoon grated Parmesan
　cheese

Yield: 6 servings

- Cook ziti according to package instructions and drain.
- Preheat oven to 350 degrees.
- Stir together spaghetti sauce, ziti, turkey and ½ cup mozzarella cheese in 2-quart casserole dish.
- Sprinkle with remaining mozzarella cheese and Parmesan cheese.
- Bake, uncovered, for 30 minutes or until bubbling.
- *Note:* Chicken may be substituted for turkey.
- *Wine Suggestion:* Italian Merlot

White Sauce Lasagna

Contributed by Donna Kelloway

Yield: 8 servings

3 whole chicken breasts, halved

1¼ cups chicken broth

1 cup water

1 pound lasagna noodles

¾ cup butter

½ cup all-purpose flour

3½ cups half and half

½ teaspoon rosemary

½ teaspoon tarragon

½ teaspoon Beau Monde Seasoning (recipe follows)

½ teaspoon salt

Dash of nutmeg

1½ cups grated Parmesan cheese

1 cup chopped parsley, divided

¼ pound prosciutto ham, shredded

- Cook chicken in broth and water for 30 minutes or until tender. Reserve 1 cup broth.
- Cool chicken, bone and cut into bite-sized strips.
- Cook lasagna noodles *al dente*. Drain and dry on towels.
- Preheat oven to 350 degrees.
- Melt butter in large saucepan. Blend in flour and cook over medium heat for 3 minutes, stirring constantly.
- Add half and half and broth, and bring to a boil over low heat, stirring constantly with wire whisk. Add seasonings, cheese and ½ cup parsley.
- Alternate layers of noodles, sauce, chicken and ham in lightly greased 9x13-inch pan, ending with noodles and sauce.
- Bake for 20 to 25 minutes. Top with remaining parsley.
- *Wine Suggestion:* Italian Valpolicella

Beau Monde Seasoning

1 tablespoon ground celery seed

¼ cup salt

3 tablespoons sugar

4 teaspoons onion powder

Yield: ½ cup

- Mix all ingredients together.
- Store in airtight container.

Chickenini

Contributed by Donna Robbins

Yield: 6 servings

3 whole chicken breasts, skinned, boned and halved

1 16-ounce jar spaghetti sauce

2 medium-sized zucchini, sliced

2 cups grated mozzarella cheese

1 6-ounce can pitted black olives, drained, sliced

1 pound spaghetti

Grated Parmesan cheese to taste

- Preheat oven to 350 degrees.
- Wash chicken and pat dry.
- Place chicken in lightly greased 3-quart casserole dish.
- Layer spaghetti sauce, zucchini, mozzarella cheese and olives on top of chicken.
- Bake, uncovered, for 90 minutes.
- Cook spaghetti according to package instructions.
- Drain spaghetti and place in serving dish.
- Serve chicken over spaghetti and sprinkle with grated Parmesan cheese.
- *Wine Suggestion:* Italian Chianti

Chicken Lasagna

Contributed by Sandy Pembleton

Yield: 8 servings

1   10-ounce can cream of mushroom soup

²/₃ cup milk

½ teaspoon poultry seasoning

1 teaspoon salt (optional)

8 ounces cream cheese

8 ounces small curd cottage cheese

⅓ cup minced onion

⅓ cup chopped green bell pepper

1 teaspoon parsley

4 to 6 cups cubed cooked chicken

8 ounces lasagna noodles

1 cup buttered bread crumbs

- Preheat oven to 350 degrees.
- Heat mushroom soup, milk, poultry seasoning and salt in saucepan.
- Add cream cheese and stir until smooth.
- Add cottage cheese and heat through, but do not boil. Remove from heat and set aside.
- Combine onion, green pepper, parsley and chicken in large bowl.
- Cook lasagna noodles according to package instructions and drain.
- Layer like a traditional lasagna in 9x13-inch pan, alternating noodles, cheese mixture, chicken mixture and bread crumbs. Top layers should be noodles, cheese mixture and bread crumbs.
- Bake for 30 to 40 minutes or until bubbly.
- Let stand for 10 minutes before cutting.
- *Wine Suggestion:* Italian Orvieto

Easy Chicken Tetrazzini

Contributed by Pat Locke

Yield: 6 servings

16 ounces spinach fettucini

¹/₄ cup butter

4 ounces mushrooms, sliced

6 tablespoons all-purpose flour

1 cup chicken broth

2 cups light cream

3 cups diced cooked chicken

White pepper to taste

Grated Parmesan cheese to taste

- Preheat oven to 350 degrees.
- Cook fettucini according to package instructions and drain.
- Spread fettucini in greased 9x13-inch casserole dish.
- Heat butter in saucepan, and sauté mushrooms for approximately 5 minutes.
- Stir in flour.
- Add broth and cream to mushroom mixture gradually.
- Cook over medium heat until sauce bubbles and thickens, stirring constantly.
- Add chicken to saucepan and season with pepper.
- Spoon sauce over cooked fettucini and sprinkle with Parmesan cheese.
- Bake, uncovered, for 20 to 25 minutes.
- *Wine Suggestion:* Chardonnay

Easy Spinach Lasagna

Contributed by Michelle Wright

Yield: 8 servings

1   15-ounce jar spaghetti
     sauce

2   6-ounce cans tomato paste

1 tablespoon basil

1/4 teaspoon pepper

1/2 teaspoon oregano

1/2 teaspoon minced garlic

1   10-ounce package frozen
     chopped spinach, thawed

2 eggs, beaten

16 ounces cottage or ricotta
cheese

1/2 cup grated Parmesan
cheese, divided

1/2 cup grated Romano cheese,
divided

8 ounces uncooked lasagna
noodles

8 ounces mozzarella cheese,
shredded

- Preheat oven to 350 degrees.
- Combine spaghetti sauce, tomato paste, basil, pepper, oregano and garlic. Set aside.
- Squeeze excess moisture from spinach.
- Combine eggs, cottage cheese, spinach, 1/4 cup Parmesan cheese and 1/4 cup Romano cheese. Set aside.
- Spread 1/3 of the sauce mixture on bottom of ungreased 9x13-inch baking dish.
- Place 1/3 of the uncooked lasagna noodles over sauce.
- Spread 1/3 of the spinach mixture over noodles.
- Repeat layers 2 more times.
- Sprinkle with mozzarella cheese and remaining 1/4 cup Parmesan cheese and 1/4 cup Romano cheese.
- Cover with foil and bake for 1 hour and 15 minutes.
- Let stand for 10 minutes before serving.
- *Wine Suggestion:* Italian Chianti

Greek-Style Spinach Pie

Contributed by Linda Shaffer

Yield: Variable

1   1-pound package phyllo dough

1/2 cup melted butter or margarine

1 1/2 pounds fresh spinach or 2   10-ounce packages frozen chopped spinach

1 tablespoon salt

2 eggs

2 cups small curd cottage cheese

1 cup grated feta cheese

2 green onions, minced

- Preheat oven to 350 degrees.
- Layer 10 sheets phyllo in bottom of greased 9x13-inch baking pan, basting each sheet with melted butter.
- Soak fresh spinach in pan of water with salt for 15 minutes, drain and chop coarsely.
- If using frozen spinach, cook according to package instructions, drain and squeeze out excess moisture.
- Beat eggs with fork in large bowl.
- Add cheeses and green onions to beaten eggs.
- Fold in spinach.
- Pour spinach mixture into pan.
- Layer 10 more sheets of phyllo over spinach mixture, basting each sheet with melted butter.
- Bake for 40 minutes.
- Cut into servings as follows:
  —for appetizers approximately 1 1/2-inches square
  —for side dish approximately 3-inches square
  —for main dish approximately 4 1/2-inches square
- *Wine Suggestion:* Spanish white wine

Spinach Soufflé

Contributed by Tracey Mulvaney

Yield: 4 servings

1   10-ounce package frozen spinach, thawed

3 tablespoons butter, melted

¼ cup all-purpose flour

12 ounces cottage cheese

3 ounces Cheddar, Parmesan or Swiss cheese, grated

3 eggs, beaten

- Preheat oven to 350 degrees.
- Squeeze excess moisture from spinach.
- Combine butter, flour and cheeses and add to beaten eggs.
- Fold in spinach.
- Pour into lightly greased 1½-quart casserole dish.
- Bake, uncovered, for 1 hour.

Pinachie

Contributed by Jentje Cain

Yield: 12 servings

2   10-ounce packages frozen spinach

6 eggs

1½ pounds mozzarella cheese, grated

1 clove of garlic, minced

Dash of cayenne pepper

1 teaspoon oregano

½ teaspoon basil

Salt and pepper to taste

2   9-inch pie shells, unbaked

- Preheat oven to 375 degrees.
- Cook spinach according to package instructions.
- Squeeze excess moisture from spinach.
- Combine spinach with remaining ingredients except pie shells and mix well.
- Pour mixture into 2 pie shells.
- Bake for 20 to 30 minutes or until pies are lightly browned and centers are firm.
- *Note:* Pies may be frozen either before or after baking.

New England Clam Quiche

Contributed by Tracey Mulvaney

Yield: 6 servings

1   9-inch unbaked pie shell, lightly pricked

½ pound bacon, cooked and crumbled

1   15-ounce can New England clam chowder

4 eggs, slightly beaten

½ cup finely chopped onion

½ cup plain yogurt

2 tablespoons chopped fresh parsley

¼ teaspoon pepper

4 slices American cheese

▪ Preheat oven to 400 degrees.
▪ Bake pie shell for 8 to 10 minutes. Remove pie shell from oven.
▪ Reduce oven temperature to 325 degrees.
▪ Combine bacon, chowder, eggs, onion, yogurt, parsley and pepper in bowl. Mix well.
▪ Pour ⅔ of the chowder mixture into baked pie shell.
▪ Arrange cheese slices on top of chowder mixture.
▪ Cover with remaining chowder mixture.
▪ Bake for 1 hour or until knife inserted near center of quiche comes out clean.
▪ Let stand for 20 minutes before cutting.

Pepperoni Quiche

Contributed by Sally Montigney

Yield: 10 servings

2 cups (½ pound) diced
   pepperoni

1 cup shredded mozzarella
   cheese

1 cup shredded or diced
   Muenster cheese

2 eggs, lightly beaten

2 cups milk

1½ cups all-purpose flour

- Preheat oven to 400 degrees.
- Mix all ingredients together and turn into well greased 9x13-inch baking pan.
- Bake for 15 to 20 minutes.
- Cool for 20 minutes.
- Cut into meal-sized pieces or smaller pieces to serve as hors d'oeuvres.

Spaghetti Pie

Contributed by Adele Friedrich

Yield: 6 servings

8 ounces spaghetti

2 eggs

2 tablespoons butter

⅓ cup grated Parmesan cheese

8 ounces ricotta cheese

½ pound ground beef,
   browned

1 8-ounce can tomato sauce

4 ounces mozzarella cheese,
   shredded

- Cook spaghetti according to package instructions and drain.
- Preheat oven to 350 degrees.
- Mix spaghetti with eggs, butter and Parmesan cheese.
- Make shell by patting spaghetti mixture into 9 or 10-inch pie plate, pushing up around edges to form rim.
- Spread ricotta cheese over spaghetti.
- Add ground beef, then cover with tomato sauce.
- Top with mozzarella cheese.
- Bake, uncovered, for 45 minutes.
- *Note:* A fun dinner for the kids, and adults love it, too.

Stromboli Mustone

Contributed by Julie Lowe

Yield: 4 servings

1 loaf frozen bread dough

1 10-ounce package frozen chopped spinach, thawed

½ pound Italian sausage, cooked and drained

½ pound shredded mozzarella cheese

1 egg white

1 tablespoon water

Caraway seed to taste

Tomato sauce to taste

- Let dough thaw and rise according to package instructions.
- Preheat oven to 350 degrees.
- Punch dough down and roll into 10x12-inch rectangle.
- Squeeze excess moisture from spinach.
- Combine sausage, cheese and spinach and spread over dough.
- Roll up dough lengthwise, pinching edges together.
- Place dough roll on greased baking sheet.
- Combine egg white and water and brush on dough roll.
- Sprinkle with caraway seed.
- Bake for 30 minutes or until well browned.
- Serve with tomato sauce.
- *Note:* Different combinations of filling ingredients, such as mushrooms, onions, peppers, olives, tomato sauce or different cheeses, may be used.

Lite Calzone

Contributed by Sally Van Orden

Yield: 4 servings

¹/₃ cup margarine, softened

1¹/₂ cups all-purpose flour

¹/₄ cup grated Parmesan cheese

2 teaspoons baking powder

¹/₂ teaspoon baking soda

¹/₂ cup plain yogurt

4 ounces part-skim ricotta cheese

1 egg

4 ounces mozzarella cheese, grated

Chopped parsley to taste

- Preheat oven to 400 degrees.
- Cut margarine into flour until crumbly.
- Blend in Parmesan cheese, baking powder and baking soda.
- Blend in yogurt until mixture forms a soft dough.
- Divide dough into 4 balls and set aside.
- Mix ricotta cheese, egg, mozzarella cheese and parsley in separate bowl to make filling.
- Roll each dough ball on floured surface until about ¹/₈ inch thick.
- Place ¹/₄ of the filling on each circle of dough.
- Fold dough over filling to form half circle.
- Press edges together with floured fork to seal.
- Place calzones on greased baking sheet and bake for 15 minutes.
- *Note:* These are great plain or with a little tomato sauce on top.

Chet's Old Dominion Macaroni and Cheese

Contributed by Kearsley Walsh

Yield: 6 servings

1 heaping cup macaroni

2 tablespoons butter

Dash of salt

Dash of pepper

½ tablespoon all-purpose flour

5 tablespoons Parmesan cheese

8 ounces Cheddar cheese, diced

½ cup milk

- Preheat oven to 450 degrees.
- Cook macaroni according to package instructions and rinse.
- Place macaroni in 2-quart casserole dish.
- Add butter, salt, pepper, flour, Parmesan cheese and Cheddar cheese to macaroni and stir.
- Add milk to cover macaroni.
- Place casserole dish in oven and set timer for 30 minutes. Watch casserole carefully and when macaroni begins to brown, reduce oven temperature to 350 degrees.
- Bake for remainder of 30 minute baking time.

Pierogies

Contributed by Mary Demmy

Yield: 8 servings

4 cups all-purpose flour

1 teaspoon salt

1 egg

1 cup water

1 recipe Filling (recipes on page 157)

4 quarts water

1 tablespoon salt

1 tablespoon vegetable oil

Oil for frying

- Mix flour, salt, egg and 1 cup water and knead until dough is smooth and elastic. Dough should be soft, not stiff.
- Cover dough and let rest for at least 15 minutes.
- Roll out dough on lightly floured board until 1/8 inch thick and cut into 3-inch rounds or squares.
- Place filling on rounds generously and press cut edges together to seal.
- Place pierogies on floured cloth until ready to cook.
- Fill large pot with 4 quarts water, salt and vegetable oil and bring to a boil.
- Add pierogies to pot 1 by 1, stirring, and cook until water returns to a boil and pierogies rise to the top. Drain.
- Heat oil for frying in large skillet or deep fryer.
- Drop pierogies into hot oil and cook until slightly browned. Drain on paper towels.

Cabbage Filling

1 small head cabbage, shredded

1 small onion, chopped

1/2 teaspoon salt

1/4 teaspoon pepper

1 tablespoon vegetable oil

■ Combine all ingredients in saucepan, and cook over low heat for 10 minutes, stirring often. Let cool.

Cheese Filling

1 1/2 pounds dry cottage cheese

1/2 teaspoon salt

1/2 teaspoon sugar

1 egg yolk

Chopped dill to taste

■ Drain cottage cheese.

■ Mash all ingredients together.

Potato-Cheese Filling

5 to 6 medium-sized potatoes, diced

1 tablespoon butter

3 ounces American or Cheddar cheese, cubed

■ Cook potatoes in salted water until tender and drain.

■ Mash hot potatoes with butter and cheese. Let cool.

Onion Pie

Contributed by Betty Straight

Yield: 6 servings

1 cup coarsely crumbled saltine crackers

1/2 cup melted butter

2 1/2 cups thickly sliced Vidalia onions or other onions

2 tablespoons butter

1/2 pound sliced Swiss cheese

1 teaspoon salt

Pepper to taste

1 1/2 cups milk

3 eggs, beaten

- Preheat oven to 350 degrees.
- Mix cracker crumbs and melted butter.
- Press crumb mixture into a 9-inch pie plate.
- Fry onions in butter until onions are clear.
- Cover bottom of pie plate with onions and top with cheese, salt and pepper.
- Scald milk and remove from heat.
- Stir a small amount of hot milk into beaten eggs; stir eggs into hot milk.
- Pour milk mixture into pie plate.
- Bake for 40 to 45 minutes or until browned.

Chili Rellenos Eggs

Contributed by Mary Vane

Yield: 8 servings

10 eggs

½ cup all-purpose flour

1 teaspoon baking powder

⅛ teaspoon salt

½ cup butter, melted

1 7-ounce can diced green chilies

2 cups cottage cheese

1 pound Monterey Jack cheese, shredded

- Preheat oven to 400 degrees.
- Beat eggs lightly in bowl. Add flour, baking powder and salt and blend until smooth.
- Stir melted butter, undrained chilies and cheeses into mixture and mix well.
- Pour mixture into greased 9x13-inch baking pan and bake for 15 minutes.
- Reset oven to 350 degrees and bake for 30 to 40 minutes more or until golden brown.
- Let stand for 10 to 15 minutes before serving.
- Serve hot.
- *Note:* This dish may also be baked in a jelly-roll pan, cut into squares and served as an appetizer.

Egg Soufflé

Contributed by Pat Kremer

Yield: 10 servings

6 tablespoons butter, softened

9 slices white bread, crusts trimmed

8 ounces sharp Cheddar cheese, grated

8 ounces bacon, fried until crisp and crumbled

6 eggs

3 cups milk

1/2 teaspoon salt

Pepper to taste

- Butter bread generously and cut into cubes.
- Place bread cubes in buttered 9x13-inch casserole dish.
- Sprinkle cheese over bread cubes.
- Sprinkle bacon over cheese.
- Beat eggs with milk, salt and pepper.
- Pour into casserole.
- Refrigerate overnight.
- Preheat oven to 350 degrees.
- Remove casserole from refrigerator.
- Bake for 50 minutes.
- *Note:* Chopped peppers or onions can be added for variety.

Cheese Oven Omelet

Contributed by Tracey Mulvaney

Yield: 5 servings

10 eggs

1 cup milk

1/2 teaspoon seasoned salt

1 1/2 cups shredded Cheddar or mozzarella cheese (approximately 6 ounces)

1 tablespoon instant dry minced onion

- Preheat oven to 325 degrees.
- Beat together eggs, milk and salt.
- Stir in cheese and onion.
- Pour into greased 9x13-inch baking pan.
- Bake for 40 to 45 minutes or until golden brown.

Eggs • Cheeses

Easy Cheesy Breakfast Casserole

Contributed by Michelle Wright

Yield: 10 servings

1½ pounds bulk sausage, browned and drained

12 eggs, beaten

1   12-ounce package bread cubes or stuffing

1½ teaspoons dry mustard

1 pound sharp Cheddar or Monterey Jack cheese, shredded

- Mix all ingredients in large bowl.
- Place mixture in ungreased 9x13-inch casserole dish.
- Refrigerate overnight.
- Preheat oven to 350 degrees.
- Bring casserole to room temperature. Bake for 45 minutes.
- Let cool for 10 minutes before serving.
- *Note:* Freezes well.

Puffy French Toast

Contributed by Sisi Morris

Yield: 4 servings

4 eggs, divided

½ cup pancake mix or biscuit mix

1 tablespoon milk or water

2 tablespoons packed brown sugar

Oil for frying

8 slices bread

- Beat 3 eggs in shallow dish.
- Combine pancake mix, milk, brown sugar and remaining egg in separate shallow dish and mix well to make batter.
- Pour oil into skillet to ½-inch depth and heat until hot.
- Dip each slice of bread into beaten eggs, then into batter.
- Fry battered bread in hot oil until golden brown, then turn and fry other side.
- Drain on paper towels and keep warm until all slices are cooked.
- *Note:* Serve hot with maple syrup, sausage and a cluster of grapes.

Pasta ▪ Eggs ▪ Cheeses

See also...

- Angel Hair Pasta with Shiitake Mushrooms
- Penne Arrabiate
- Risotto alla Principessa

...in the Restaurant Section

Vegetables · Side Dishes

Longwood Gardens

No visit to the area is complete without a chance to savor world-renowned Longwood Gardens' 1,050 acres and experience its breathtaking array of conservatories and outdoor gardens. Open every day of the year, Longwood is truly a garden for all seasons. In winter, 20 indoor gardens of abundant, fragrant blooms take center stage. Starting with the daffodils in March, the focus moves outside to formal gardens and spectacularly illuminated fountain displays.

Asparagus-Mushroom Casserole

Contributed by a Friend   **Yield: 6 servings**

4 cups sliced fresh mushrooms

1 cup chopped onions

¼ cup butter or margarine

2 tablespoons all-purpose flour

1 chicken bouillon cube

½ teaspoon nutmeg

Salt and pepper to taste

1 cup skim milk

1 pound fresh or frozen asparagus, cooked, drained

¼ cup chopped pimento

1½ teaspoons lemon juice

¾ cup soft bread cubes

- Preheat oven to 350 degrees.
- Sauté mushrooms and onions in 3 tablespoons butter in large skillet for 10 minutes. Remove vegetables with slotted spoon.
- Add flour, bouillon, nutmeg, salt and pepper to skillet and cook for 1 minute.
- Add milk and cook until thick and bubbly, stirring constantly.
- Stir in mushroom mixture, asparagus, pimento and lemon juice and pour into buttered 3-quart casserole dish.
- Sauté bread cubes in remaining butter. Sprinkle over top.
- Bake for 40 minutes.

Dilly Beans

Contributed by Mary Rice   **Yield: 6 servings**

1 pound fresh green beans, trimmed

¼ cup butter, melted

2 tablespoons lemon juice

1 tablespoon dill

1 clove of garlic, crushed

- Steam beans in saucepan until just tender, about 10 minutes.
- Drain beans in colander and refresh with cold water.
- Return beans to saucepan and toss with butter, lemon juice, dill and garlic.
- Reheat and serve immediately.
- *Note:* May be prepared ahead and microwaved before serving.

Green Beans in Lemon-Cream Sauce

Contributed by Didi Lovett

Yield: 6 servings

1½ pounds green beans, trimmed

¾ cup heavy cream, divided

¼ cup butter

1 egg

Salt and pepper to taste

¼ teaspoon nutmeg

2 tablespoons freshly grated Parmesan cheese

Juice of 1 lemon

- Cook beans in large saucepan in salted water until tender-crisp, drain and return to saucepan.

- Set aside 2 tablespoons heavy cream.

- Add butter and remaining heavy cream to saucepan and cook over medium heat just until butter is melted.

- Combine egg, reserved heavy cream, salt, pepper, nutmeg and Parmesan cheese in small bowl.

- Add lemon juice to egg mixture, beat well and pour mixture over beans.

- Cook for 2 to 3 minutes or until sauce thickens and coats beans, stirring constantly.

- *Note:* May be prepared up to 1 day ahead and reheated in microwave.

Broccoli with Shrimp Sauce

Contributed by Jennifer Ray Simonton

Yield: 4 servings

1   10-ounce can cream of shrimp soup

1   4-ounce package cream cheese with chives

1 teaspoon lemon juice

1/4 cup milk

1 large head broccoli, steamed

- Place soup, cream cheese, lemon juice and milk in double boiler and heat slowly, stirring mixture frequently until boiling.
- Serve over broccoli.
- *Note:* Asparagus may be substituted for broccoli in this colorful dish.

Broccoli Casserole

Contributed by Susan Kremer

Yield: 8 servings

6 cups fresh broccoli

1   10-ounce can cream of mushroom soup

1 cup shredded Cheddar cheese, divided

1/4 cup milk

1/4 cup mayonnaise

2 eggs, beaten

1 teaspoon lemon juice

Salt and pepper to taste

3/4 cup Ritz cracker crumbs

- Preheat oven to 350 degrees.
- Cook broccoli in a small amount of water until tender and drain well.
- Spread broccoli over bottom of 2-quart casserole dish.
- Mix soup, 1/2 cup cheese, milk, mayonnaise, eggs, lemon juice, salt and pepper in large bowl.
- Pour mixture over broccoli.
- Sprinkle remaining cheese over mixture.
- Sprinkle cracker crumbs over top of cheese.
- Bake, uncovered, for 45 minutes.
- *Note:* May substitute crouton crumbs for Ritz cracker crumbs.

Spicy Spinach

Contributed by Mary Rice

Yield: 6 servings

2   10-ounce packages frozen chopped spinach

¼ cup butter

2 tablespoons all-purpose flour

2 tablespoons chopped onion

½ cup evaporated milk or light cream

1 clove of garlic, minced

1 teaspoon salt

4 ounces Monterey Jack cheese, shredded

4 ounces Monterey Jack cheese with jalapeños, shredded

1 teaspoon Worcestershire sauce

- Cook spinach according to package instructions, drain and reserve ½ cup spinach liquid.
- Preheat oven to 350 degrees.
- Melt butter in saucepan.
- Add flour to saucepan and cook over medium heat for 2 minutes, stirring constantly, but do not brown.
- Add onion, reserved spinach liquid and evaporated milk and cook until bubbly, stirring constantly.
- Add garlic, salt, cheeses and Worcestershire sauce, and stir until cheeses melt.
- Add spinach, stir, and turn into buttered 2-quart casserole dish.
- Bake for 15 minutes.
- *Note:* May be prepared ahead and baked just before serving.

Eggplant with Tomato and Mozzarella

Contributed by Sharon Rolle

Yield: 4 servings

1½ pounds eggplant, peeled

Salt

½ cup olive oil, divided

1 small onion, chopped

1 clove of garlic, minced

1 pound tomatoes, chopped

2 tablespoons chopped fresh basil

2 teaspoons dried basil

Salt and pepper to taste

Pinch of sugar

8 ounces ½-inch wide noodles, cooked according to package instructions and drained

½ pound mozzarella cheese, shredded

½ pound salami, diced

½ cup grated Parmesan cheese, divided

- Slice eggplant into ½-inch slices, sprinkle with salt and let stand for 30 minutes.
- Preheat oven to 375 degrees.
- Rinse eggplant slices and pat dry.
- Sauté eggplant slices in ⅓ cup olive oil in large skillet until golden brown.
- Drain eggplant slices on paper towels.
- Mix remaining oil, onion, garlic, tomatoes, fresh basil, dried basil, salt, pepper and sugar in same skillet and cook, covered, for 10 minutes.
- Add cooked noodles, mozzarella cheese, salami and half the Parmesan cheese to tomato mixture.
- Layer eggplant slices in 9x13-inch baking pan and top with noodle and tomato mixture.
- Season with salt and pepper and top with remaining Parmesan cheese.
- Bake for 25 minutes.

Carrots for Color

Contributed by Didi Lovett

Yield: 6 servings

1 orange

½ cup sugar

1 tablespoon cornstarch

½ cup cider vinegar

2 tablespoons water

2 pounds carrots, sliced and cooked until just tender

3 tablespoons butter

- Grate rind of orange and set aside.
- Squeeze juice from orange and set aside.
- Combine sugar, cornstarch, vinegar and water in saucepan.
- Bring mixture to a boil, stirring constantly until thickened and clear.
- Stir orange rind and orange juice into thickened mixture.
- Add carrots and butter and toss until carrots are well coated.
- *Note:* This recipe may be prepared a day or 2 ahead. Decorate with mint leaves or watercress for added color. Even those who never eat carrots will enjoy this dish.

Cheesy Squash Casserole

Contributed by Connie Greendoner

Yield: 8 servings

12 small to medium-sized summer squash

6 slices bacon

3/4 cup chopped onion

3 eggs, beaten

1 1/2 cups shredded Cheddar cheese

Salt and pepper to taste

1 1/2 teaspoons Worcestershire sauce

- Preheat oven to 350 degrees.
- Cook squash in a small amount of water until tender, drain and mash. Set aside in large bowl and let cool.
- Fry bacon until crisp and drain, reserving bacon fat. Crumble bacon and add to cooled squash.
- Sauté onion in bacon fat. Drain fat and add onion to squash mixture.
- Add remaining ingredients to squash mixture, mix well, and pour into 1 1/2-quart casserole dish.
- Bake, uncovered, for 30 minutes.
- *Note:* Acorn, butternut, or other winter squash are also delicious in this dish.

Baked Onions with Cheese

Contributed by Joan Long

Yield: 6 servings

1½ pounds onions, thinly sliced

3 tablespoons butter

½ cup milk

4 ounces sharp cheese, shredded

Paprika to taste

½ cup bread crumbs

- Preheat oven to 375 degrees.
- Cook sliced onions in boiling salted water to cover for 8 minutes and drain well.
- Sauté onions in butter until straw-colored.
- Add milk, cheese and paprika and stir until cheese is melted.
- Pour mixture into 2-quart casserole dish.
- Sprinkle with bread crumbs and paprika.
- Bake, uncovered, for 30 minutes.

Barbecued Onions

Contributed by Michelle Wright

Yield: 10 servings

½ cup cider vinegar

½ cup white vinegar

⅔ cup vegetable oil

2 teaspoons Worcestershire sauce

2 to 3 cloves of garlic, minced

½ teaspoon paprika

3 tablespoons catsup

½ teaspoon dry mustard

Tabasco sauce to taste

6 large Vidalia onions, sliced

- Mix all ingredients except onions in blender to form marinade.
- Combine sliced onions and marinade and refrigerate for 6 to 8 hours.
- Place onions with a small amount of sauce in aluminum foil and grill for 30 minutes on low heat.

Jiffy Tomato Stack-Ups

Contributed by Sharon Rolle

Yield: 4 servings

1 10-ounce package chopped broccoli

1 cup shredded Swiss cheese

1/4 cup finely chopped onion

4 large tomatoes

- Cook broccoli according to package instructions and drain.
- Combine broccoli, cheese and onion in bowl.
- Cut tomatoes into 1/2-inch thick slices and place on baking sheet.
- Top each tomato slice with broccoli mixture.
- Broil 3 to 5 inches from heat source for 8 minutes or until cheese melts.

Vegetable Casserole

Contributed by Nancy Graves

Yield: 8 servings

1 10-ounce package frozen tiny peas

1 10-ounce package frozen lima beans

1 10-ounce package frozen French-style green beans

1 cup mayonnaise

1 small onion, grated

Tabasco sauce to taste

2 hard-boiled eggs, sieved

1 tablespoon Worcestershire sauce

1 teaspoon mustard

- Preheat oven to 350 degrees.
- Cook each frozen vegetable according to package instructions and drain.
- Mix vegetables together in 2-quart casserole dish.
- Mix mayonnaise, onion, Tabasco sauce, eggs, Worcestershire sauce and mustard in small bowl and pour over vegetables. Mix together.
- Bake, uncovered, for 20 to 30 minutes.
- *Note:* May be prepared ahead.

Vegetable Fantasia

Contributed by Mary Vane, Julie Lowe

Yield: 10 servings

4   10-ounce packages chopped broccoli

½ pound mushrooms, sliced

¼ cup plus 2 tablespoons butter, divided

½ cup mayonnaise

½ cup sour cream

½ cup Parmesan cheese

1   14-ounce can artichoke hearts, drained (not marinated)

Salt and pepper to taste

3 tomatoes, sliced ½ inch thick

½ cup dry bread crumbs

- Preheat oven to 325 degrees.
- Cook broccoli according to package instructions and drain.
- Sauté sliced mushrooms in 2 tablespoons butter.
- Combine mayonnaise, sour cream and Parmesan cheese in bowl.
- Stir in artichoke hearts, broccoli, mushrooms, salt and pepper.
- Pour mixture into greased 9x13-inch casserole dish.
- Arrange sliced tomatoes over broccoli mixture.
- Sauté bread crumbs in remaining butter until brown.
- Sprinkle bread crumbs over casserole.
- Bake, uncovered, for 20 minutes.
- *Note:* May be prepared ahead. Spinach may be substituted for broccoli.

Four Friends Summer Veggies

Contributed by Gay Ann Reilly

Yield: 6 servings

1 medium-sized onion, sliced

1 eggplant, diced

¼ cup olive oil

4 to 5 zucchini, sliced

2 cups tomatoes, diced

1 medium-sized green bell pepper, diced

1 teaspoon garlic salt

1 teaspoon Maggi

1 teaspoon Tabasco sauce

1 teaspoon Accent (optional)

½ cup wine vinegar

1 teaspoon basil

1 teaspoon thyme

1 to 2 bay leaves

Pepper to taste

- Preheat oven to 350 degrees.
- Sauté onion and eggplant in olive oil.
- Add zucchini, tomatoes and green pepper.
- Season with garlic salt, Maggi, Tabasco sauce, Accent, vinegar, basil, thyme, bay leaves and pepper.
- Sauté mixture for 15 to 20 minutes. Remove bay leaf.
- Pour into 2-quart casserole dish and top with dab of olive oil.
- Bake, uncovered, for 15 to 20 minutes.
- *Note:* The four friends are garlic salt, Maggi, Tabasco sauce and Accent.

Parmesan Potato Fingers

Contributed by Patti Snow

Yield: 10 servings

1/4 cup all-purpose flour

1/4 cup grated Parmesan cheese

2 tablespoons parsley flakes

3/4 teaspoon salt

1/8 teaspoon pepper

6 medium-sized potatoes, cut into eighths lengthwise

1/3 cup margarine

- Preheat oven to 375 degrees.
- Combine flour, cheese, parsley, salt and pepper in plastic bag.
- Drop potato strips a few at a time into flour mixture and shake to coat.
- Melt margarine in shallow 11x15-inch baking pan.
- Place potato strips in single layer in pan.
- Bake, uncovered, for 1 hour, turning potatoes after 30 minutes.
- Serve immediately.
- *Note:* Potatoes may be peeled or left unpeeled.

Lovey's Potatoes

Contributed by Kearsley Walsh

Yield: 6 servings

1 onion, chopped

1/4 cup butter

2 cups sour cream

1   10-ounce can cream of chicken soup

Salt and pepper to taste

1   20-ounce package frozen hashed brown potatoes, thawed

6 ounces Cheddar cheese, grated

- Preheat oven to 350 degrees.
- Sauté onion in butter.
- Mix onion, sour cream and chicken soup in large bowl.
- Season with salt and pepper.
- Add thawed potatoes and stir.
- Pour mixture into 9x13-inch casserole dish.
- Sprinkle with grated cheese.
- Bake, uncovered, for 50 minutes.

Sausage Stuffing Casserole

Contributed by
Mrs. Edgar S. Woolard, Jr.

Yield: 12 servings

1 pound highly seasoned
  sausage

1 cup chopped celery

½ cup chopped onion

6 cups seasoned stuffing,
  divided

1 10-ounce can cream of
  mushroom soup

⅓ cup milk

- Preheat oven to 425 degrees.
- Combine sausage, celery and onion in large skillet and cook until sausage is brown. Drain fat.
- Add 3 cups stuffing to skillet, stir and set aside.
- Heat soup and milk in large pot.
- Add remaining stuffing to pot and stir to mix well.
- Add sausage mixture to pot and fold in well.
- Turn mixture into buttered 9x13-inch baking dish.
- Bake, covered, for 20 minutes.
- Cut into squares and serve hot.
- *Note:* Delicious with Thanksgiving turkey. May be frozen for up to 2 weeks prior to baking. To prepare frozen casserole, thaw and bake as directed in recipe.

Mushroom Pilaf

Contributed by Joan Long

Yield: 8 servings

¼ cup margarine, melted

1½ cups rice, uncooked

1 10-ounce can beef consommé

1 10-ounce can onion soup

½ pound fresh mushrooms, sliced

1 cup shredded Cheddar cheese

- Preheat oven to 375 degrees.
- Place melted margarine in 2-quart casserole dish.
- Add rice and stir.
- Add soups and mushrooms and stir briskly.
- Bake, covered, for 1 hour or until liquid is absorbed.
- Sprinkle cheese on top and melt under broiler.

Noodle Kugel

Contributed by Debbie Talbert

Yield: 10 servings

1 pound medium-sized egg noodles

2 cups butter

8 ounces cream cheese

1 pound cottage cheese

2 cups sour cream

1 cup white raisins

1¼ cups sugar

5 eggs, beaten

½ cup light cream

Cinnamon to taste

- Preheat oven to 325 degrees.
- Cook noodles according to package instructions and drain.
- Combine hot noodles, butter and cream cheese in large bowl and stir until melted and well blended.
- Add remaining ingredients to bowl and stir well.
- Turn into greased 3-quart casserole dish.
- Bake for 1½ hours.

Sweet Potato-Pineapple Casserole

Contributed by Valerie Trammel

Yield: 12 servings

3¹/₂ pounds (6 medium-sized) sweet potatoes or yams

¹/₂ cup butter or margarine, room temperature

1 cup sugar

1   13-ounce can evaporated milk

6 eggs

1 teaspoon salt

¹/₂ teaspoon cinnamon

¹/₂ teaspoon vanilla extract

¹/₄ teaspoon nutmeg

1   20-ounce can crushed pineapple, drained

1 cup raisins

1¹/₂ cups miniature marshmallows (optional)

- Boil sweet potatoes in salted water to cover until tender. Drain and peel.
- Break up sweet potatoes and place in large mixer bowl. Add next 8 ingredients. Beat at low speed and then at high speed, until mixture is fluffy.
- Stir in pineapple and raisins.
- Pour mixture into greased 3-quart baking dish.
- Preheat oven to 375 degrees.
- Bake, uncovered, for 20 minutes.
- Reduce heat to 350 degrees, top with marshmallows and bake for 40 minutes more.
- Remove from oven and let stand in warm place for 20 to 30 minutes before serving.

Hot Pineapple Soufflé

Contributed by Doris Kremer

Yield: 6 servings

¹/₂ cup margarine, melted

5 slices white bread, cubed

3 eggs, beaten

¹/₂ cup sugar

1   20-ounce can crushed pineapple

Nutmeg to taste

- Preheat oven to 350 degrees.
- Combine all ingredients except nutmeg and pour into buttered 2-quart casserole dish.
- Sprinkle with nutmeg.
- Bake, uncovered, for 40 minutes.

Vegetables • Side Dishes

See also...

- Italian-Style Mushroom Casserole
- Roquefort Bliss Potatoes

...in the Restaurant Section

Desserts · Sweets

Brandywine Valley Gardens

Wilmington's moderate climate is ideal for gardening. In addition to the many public gardens, private gardens are abundant. Local horticulturists and garden enthusiasts look forward to Garden Day held annually on the first Saturday of May. On this day many private gardens open their gates so that all may enjoy the blooms of spring.

Ma's Apple Strudel

Contributed by a Friend

Yield: 6 servings

⅓ cup sugar

½ teaspoon cinnamon

¼ teaspoon ground cloves

½ cup plus 1 teaspoon water, divided

4 large apples, peeled, cored and sliced

2 tablespoons cornstarch

¼ cup cold water

1 egg, beaten

1 teaspoon confectioners' sugar

1 sheet puff pastry (½ pound), thawed

- Preheat oven to 375 degrees.
- Combine sugar, cinnamon, cloves and ½ cup water in saucepan.
- Add apples and cook, covered, over medium heat for 5 minutes.
- Dissolve cornstarch in cold water.
- Stir cornstarch mixture into apple mixture.
- Cook until thickened. Let cool thoroughly.
- Combine egg, confectioners' sugar and 1 teaspoon water.
- Roll pastry on lightly floured surface to form a 12x12-inch square.
- Place apple mixture in center of square.
- Brush pastry edges with egg mixture.
- Fold pastry over filling and seal edges.
- Brush top and sides of pastry with egg mixture.
- Bake for 20 to 25 minutes or until golden brown.
- *Note:* Tart apples, such as MacIntosh or Granny Smith, are recommended.

Apple Crisp

Contributed by Basil R. Battaglia

Yield: 6 servings

4 cups peeled, cored and sliced cooking apples (such as MacIntosh or Granny Smith)

½ cup all-purpose flour

½ cup packed brown sugar

¼ cup butter

1 teaspoon cinnamon

- Preheat oven to 375 degrees.
- Place apples in a 9-inch pie plate.
- Combine flour, brown sugar, butter and cinnamon in large bowl and mix with pastry blender or fingers.
- Spread mixture over apples.
- Bake for 30 minutes.
- Serve hot or cold.
- *Note:* Top with a dollop of sour cream or whipped cream, or a scoop of vanilla ice cream.

Baked Apricots

Contributed by Anne Noble

Yield: 12 servings

½ cup butter, melted

2   28-ounce cans apricots, drained

2 cups packed brown sugar

2 cups crushed Ritz crackers

- Preheat oven to 350 degrees.
- Place ⅓ of the melted butter in 3-quart casserole dish.
- Layer apricots, brown sugar, crushed crackers and remaining butter, ½ at a time, in casserole dish.
- Bake, uncovered, for 1 hour.
- Serve hot.
- *Note:* May also be served as a side dish with ham or turkey.

Bananas Flambé

Contributed by Peter Bordi

Yield: 2 servings

2 tablespoons butter

2 slightly green bananas, sliced

2 tablespoons honey

2 tablespoons white rum

2 tablespoons Crème de Cacao

2 scoops vanilla ice cream

- Melt butter in sauté pan.
- Add bananas to pan and sauté for 1 minute. Add honey and sauté for 1 minute.
- Add rum and Crème de Cacao and heat to almost boiling.
- Ignite fumes and burn for 1 minute. Serve over ice cream.

Cherry-Oat Cobbler

Contributed by Nina Sneeringer

Yield: 8 servings

1 1/4 cups rolled oats

1/2 cup sugar, divided

1/3 cup butter, melted

1/2 cup raspberry preserves

8 ounces cream cheese, softened

1 egg

1   21-ounce can cherry pie filling

- Preheat oven to 400 degrees.
- Combine rolled oats, 1/4 cup sugar and melted butter.
- Spread in lightly greased pie plate to form shell. Bake for 10 minutes or until light brown.
- Remove from oven and let cool.
- Spread shell with preserves.
- Reduce oven temperature to 350 degrees.
- Cream together cream cheese and remaining 1/4 cup sugar. Blend in egg.
- Pour cream cheese mixture into pie shell and bake for 10 minutes.
- Remove from oven and pour cherry pie filling gently over top.
- Bake for 5 to 7 minutes.
- Chill before serving.

Four-Fruit Delight

Contributed by Mary Straight

Yield: 10 servings

1 pound pitted prunes

1 4-ounce can pineapple chunks and juice

1⅓ cups dried apricots

1 21-ounce can cherry pie filling

½ cup Sherry

1 cup water

- Preheat oven to 350 degrees.
- Layer fruit in 8-inch square baking dish, ending with cherry pie filling.
- Combine Sherry and water and pour over fruit.
- Bake, uncovered, for 1 hour.
- *Note:* Delicious served from a chafing dish as a flaming dessert by substituting Kirsch for Sherry and topping each serving with vanilla ice cream. Also great with ham or fowl as side dish.

Texas Peach Cobbler

Contributed by Mary Demmy

Yield: 6 servings

¼ cup margarine, melted

1 cup sugar

1 cup all-purpose flour

1 cup milk

1 teaspoon baking powder

2 1-pound cans sliced peaches or 6 to 8 fresh peaches, peeled and sliced

1 teaspoon cinnamon

- Preheat oven to 350 degrees.
- Mix together margarine, sugar, flour, milk and baking powder with wire whisk and pour into a greased 9x9-inch baking pan.
- Place peaches on top and sprinkle with cinnamon.
- Bake for 1 hour.
- Serve warm.
- *Note:* Delicious with vanilla ice cream.

Apple Toss Cake

Contributed by Virginia Wood

Yield: 12 servings

½ cup margarine

2 eggs

1 teaspoon vanilla extract

1½ cups all-purpose flour

1¼ cups sugar

½ teaspoon salt

1 teaspoon baking soda

1 teaspoon baking powder

1 teaspoon cinnamon

4 cups diced apples

½ cup chopped walnuts

- Preheat oven to 350 degrees.
- Melt margarine and set aside.
- Beat eggs and vanilla in small bowl and set aside.
- Sift together flour, sugar, salt, baking soda, baking powder and cinnamon in large bowl.
- Add melted margarine and egg mixture to flour mixture and blend with wooden spoon.
- Add apples and walnuts.
- Spread batter in greased and floured 9x13-inch cake pan. Batter will be stiff and form a thin layer.
- Bake for 40 minutes.
- *Note:* Delicious served warm with vanilla ice cream.

Easy Carrot Cake

Contributed by Barbara McCain

Yield: 15 servings

2 cups all-purpose flour

2 cups sugar

1 cup oil

3 cups shredded carrots

1 cup chopped pecans

½ cup raisins

1 teaspoon vanilla extract

2 teaspoons baking soda

1 teaspoon baking powder

1 teaspoon salt

4 eggs

1 teaspoon cinnamon

Cream Cheese Frosting
  (recipe follows)

- Preheat oven to 350 degrees.
- Combine all ingredients except frosting and mix well.
- Pour mixture into greased tube pan.
- Bake for 40 minutes.
- Cool for 10 minutes in pan, then invert onto serving plate.
- Cool completely, then frost with Cream Cheese Frosting.
- *Note:* A delicious moist cake, sure to bring rave reviews.

Cream Cheese Frosting

6 tablespoons butter, softened

8 ounces cream cheese, softened

1 pound (3¾ cups) confectioners' sugar

1 teaspoon vanilla extract

- Cream together butter and cream cheese in large bowl.
- Add confectioners' sugar and vanilla and blend until smooth.

All-American Three-Layer Chocolate Cake

Contributed by Mary Rice   **Yield: 16 servings**

1 cup baking cocoa	1 cup butter, softened
2 cups boiling water	2½ cups sugar
2¾ cups all-purpose flour	4 eggs
2 teaspoons baking soda	1 teaspoon vanilla extract
½ teaspoon baking powder	Chocolate Frosting (recipe follows)
½ teaspoon salt	

- Preheat oven to 350 degrees.
- Combine cocoa and boiling water and set aside to cool.
- Sift flour, baking soda, baking powder and salt together and set aside.
- Cream butter and sugar until light and fluffy in large bowl.
- Add eggs and vanilla to butter mixture and beat well.
- Add flour mixture to butter mixture alternately with chocolate mixture, beginning and ending with flour mixture, beating well after each addition.
- Grease three 9-inch cake pans and line bottoms with waxed paper circles cut to fit. Grease waxed paper and dust with flour.
- Pour batter into prepared pans and bake for 25 to 30 minutes or until layers spring back when pressed lightly.
- Cool cake layers in pans for 10 minutes, then remove from pans, peel off waxed paper, and cool completely on wire racks.
- Frost with Chocolate Frosting.

Chocolate Frosting

12 ounces semisweet chocolate, chopped
¾ cup evaporated milk or light cream
1½ cups butter
1 pound (3¾ cups) confectioners' sugar, sifted

- Heat chocolate, milk and butter in saucepan over medium heat, stirring until smooth.
- Remove from heat and whisk in confectioners' sugar until smooth.
- Place saucepan in bowl of ice and stir until frosting is of spreading consistency.

Dark Chocolate Cake with White Chocolate Buttercream Frosting

Contributed by Nancy Hyland　　　**Yield: 12 servings**

2 cups sifted all-purpose flour

¼ teaspoon salt

¼ teaspoon freshly grated nutmeg

1½ teaspoons baking soda

4 ounces unsweetened chocolate

1 cup unsalted butter, softened

1¾ cups sugar

4 eggs

1⅓ cups buttermilk

1 teaspoon vanilla extract

White Chocolate Buttercream Frosting (recipe on page 191)

- Preheat oven to 325 degrees with shelf positioned in lower third of oven.
- Sift together flour, salt, nutmeg and baking soda and set aside.
- Melt unsweetened chocolate in top of double boiler over hot, but not boiling, water.
- Remove chocolate from heat and stir until smooth. Let cool.
- Cream butter and sugar until light and fluffy, stopping mixer to scrape bowl and beaters several times.
- Add eggs 1 at a time, beating after each addition.
- Add flour mixture and buttermilk alternately to batter, beginning and ending with flour mixture and mixing well after each addition.
- Stir in vanilla and cooled chocolate, blending until color is even.
- Pour batter into two 9-inch round cake pans lined with parchment paper.
- Smooth batter level, then spread batter slightly from center toward edge of pan so cake will rise evenly.
- Bake for 35 to 45 minutes or until top is lightly springy to the touch and cake tester inserted near center comes out clean.
- Remove layers from pans and cool completely on wire racks.
- Prepare frosting.
- Place bottom layer on serving plate and cover with frosting.
- Place second layer on top and frost top and side of cake with remaining frosting.

White Chocolate Buttercream Frosting

6 tablespoons heavy cream

4 ounces white chocolate, finely chopped

1/4 cup white Crème de Cacao

1 cup unsalted butter

4 cups confectioners' sugar

- Bring cream to a boil in small saucepan.
- Pour hot cream over chopped white chocolate and stir until completely smooth.
- Stir Crème de Cacao into white chocolate mixture. Cool, stirring occasionally.
- Cream butter in large bowl.
- Add confectioners' sugar to bowl and beat for 5 minutes until light and fluffy.
- Add white chocolate mixture to butter mixture gradually, beating at low speed until desired consistency is reached.
- *Note:* This cake is beautiful decorated with dark chocolate rosettes or shavings.

Chocolate Nut Cake

Contributed by Jane Martin

Yield: 12 servings

6 eggs, separated

1¼ cups sugar

1 cup unsweetened chestnut purée

½ cup ground almonds or walnuts

1 teaspoon vanilla extract

Pinch of salt

Chocolate Mousse Frosting (recipe follows)

- Preheat oven to 325 degrees.
- Beat egg yolks and sugar in large bowl. Add chestnut purée, almonds and vanilla and mix well. Set aside.
- Beat egg whites and salt in separate bowl until stiff peaks form.
- Fold ¼ of the egg whites into chestnut mixture.
- Fold in remaining egg whites gently so mixture does not collapse.
- Pour mixture into 2 well greased and floured 9-inch cake pans.
- Bake for 35 minutes.
- Cool in pan for 15 minutes, then turn out onto wire racks to cool completely.
- Frost with Chocolate Mousse Frosting.
- *Note:* This cake is delicate and requires gentle handling. Frosting will cover any errors.

Chocolate Mousse Frosting

8 ounces semisweet chocolate

1½ cups heavy cream

- Heat chocolate and cream in saucepan over moderate heat until chocolate is melted completely.
- Pour mixture into mixer bowl and chill until slightly thick.
- Beat mixture until stiff.

Hot Fudge Sundae Cake

Contributed by Mary Rice

Yield: 6 servings

1 cup all-purpose flour

3/4 cup sugar

6 tablespoons baking cocoa, divided

2 teaspoons baking powder

1/4 teaspoon salt

2 tablespoons vegetable oil

1/2 cup milk

1 teaspoon vanilla extract

1 cup packed brown sugar

1 3/4 cups hot water

6 scoops vanilla ice cream

- Preheat oven to 350 degrees.
- Combine flour, sugar, 2 table-spoons cocoa, baking powder, salt and oil in ungreased 8-inch square pan.
- Add milk and vanilla and stir thoroughly with fork until smooth.
- Sprinkle brown sugar and remaining cocoa over chocolate mixture.
- Pour hot water over mixture. Do not stir.
- Bake for 40 minutes.
- Remove pan from oven and spoon cake onto serving plates.
- Top cake with ice cream and hot syrup from bottom of pan.
- Serve immediately.
- *Note:* Kids love to prepare this delicious treat.

Glazed Chocolate Torte

Contributed by Betty Snyder   **Yield: 8 servings**

¾ cup unsalted butter, softened

⅓ cup sugar

5 egg yolks

6 ounces semisweet chocolate, melted

¾ cup all-purpose flour

6 egg whites

Pinch of salt

6 tablespoons apricot preserves

Chocolate Glaze (recipe on page 195)

Marzipan Violets with Chocolate Leaves (recipe on page 195)

Sweetened whipped cream to taste

- Preheat oven to 350 degrees.
- Cream butter and sugar in large bowl.
- Add yolks to butter mixture and beat well. Stir in melted chocolate.
- Add flour and stir until just combined. Set aside.
- Combine egg whites with salt and beat until firm, but not stiff or dry.
- Stir ¼ of the egg whites into chocolate mixture and mix well.
- Fold remaining egg whites, in several additions, gently into chocolate mixture.
- Pour mixture into buttered and waxed paper-lined 8-inch springform pan and level top.
- Bake for 45 to 50 minutes or until top springs back when pressed lightly.
- Cool cake in pan for 10 minutes, then remove side of pan. Let cool completely.
- Cover cooled cake and let stand overnight, or freeze.
- Strain apricot preserves into small saucepan and bring to a boil.
- Pour boiling preserves over cake and smooth top with spatula.
- Pour Chocolate Glaze onto center of cake and smooth top with spatula. Allow thin coating to run down side of cake.
- Allow cake to stand for 1 hour or until glaze sets.
- Decorate with Marzipan Violets with Chocolate Leaves.
- Garnish with whipped cream before serving.

Chocolate Glaze

¼ cup light corn syrup

3 tablespoons water

2 tablespoons butter, cut into pieces

1½ cups semisweet chocolate chips

- Bring corn syrup, water and butter to a boil in saucepan.
- Remove from heat and add chocolate chips. Stir until melted.
- Let mixture stand until thickened and cooled to room temperature, stirring occasionally.

Marzipan Violets with Chocolate Leaves

½ egg white

½ cup almond paste

¾ cup sifted confectioners' sugar

Lemon juice

Purple and yellow food coloring, diluted

2   1-ounce squares semisweet chocolate

Fresh green leaves with stems

- Whip egg white in small bowl until fluffy.
- Work almond paste into egg white gradually with hands or back of spoon.
- Add confectioners' sugar and blend until mixture forms a paste, adding lemon juice if mixture is too thick.
- Knead paste until smooth and easy to handle, placing bowl over ice if paste becomes oily.
- Form paste into small petals and press several petals together at their base to form violets. Form tiny balls of paste and place in centers of violets.
- Paint violet petals with purple food coloring and centers with yellow food coloring with pastry brush.
- Store violets in covered container in cool place until ready to use.
- Melt chocolate in top of double boiler over low heat. Spread underside of leaves almost to edge with chocolate.
- Chill for 1 to 2 minutes or until chocolate is firm.
- Peel leaves away from chocolate starting at stem. Store, covered, in refrigerator or freezer. Use at room temperature.
- Spray leaves with nonstick cooking spray for a shiny finish.

Feather-Light Cocoa Cake

Contributed by Beth Ann Wahl

Yield: 8 servings

8 egg whites, divided, room temperature

1 cup sugar

½ cup baking cocoa

3 tablespoons vegetable oil

½ cup almonds, very finely chopped

½ cup walnuts, very finely chopped

Confectioners' sugar for dusting

Fresh strawberries or raspberries for garnish

- Preheat oven to 350 degrees.
- Beat 6 egg whites in large bowl with electric mixer until stiff and dry. Set aside.
- Combine sugar, cocoa, oil and remaining egg whites in separate large bowl.
- Add chopped nuts to cocoa mixture and mix well.
- Mix ¼ of the beaten egg whites into cocoa mixture gently. Add remaining egg whites and fold until no white appears.
- Pour batter into greased and floured 9-inch springform pan.
- Bake for 30 to 35 minutes or until center is firm.
- Cool cake in pan.
- Remove cake from pan, dust with confectioners' sugar and garnish with fruit.
- *Note:* For a more elegant appearance, place a paper doily over baked cake, sprinkle with confectioners' sugar and remove doily carefully.

Lynn's Double-Fudge Chocolate Cake

Contributed by Karen Lazar

Yield: 12 servings

1 cup sugar

1/2 cup butter

4 eggs

1 teaspoon vanilla extract

Pinch of salt

1 teaspoon baking powder

1 cup cake flour

1 16-ounce can chocolate syrup

Frosting (recipe follows)

- Preheat oven to 350 degrees.
- Cream sugar and butter in large bowl.
- Add eggs 1 at a time, beating after each addition.
- Add vanilla.
- Mix salt, baking powder and flour in separate bowl.
- Add chocolate syrup and flour mixture alternately to sugar mixture, blending thoroughly after each addition.
- Pour into greased and floured 9x13-inch cake pan.
- Bake for 30 minutes.
- Allow cake to cool completely, then frost in pan.

Frosting

1 cup sugar

1/2 cup butter

1/3 cup evaporated milk

1/3 cup chocolate chips

- Heat sugar, butter and evaporated milk in saucepan over medium heat until sugar is melted.
- Remove saucepan from heat and stir in chocolate chips.
- Let cool to spreading consistency.

Fresh Coconut Cake

Contributed by Joan Connolly

Yield: 15 servings

6 eggs

2 cups sugar

1/2 cup butter

1 cup hot milk

2 1/2 cups sifted all-purpose flour

1 teaspoon vanilla extract

1 tablespoon baking powder

1/2 cup chopped black walnuts (optional)

Coconut Frosting (recipe follows)

1 1/2 cups freshly grated coconut

- Preheat oven to 350 degrees.
- Separate 2 eggs. Reserve whites for frosting.
- Beat separated egg yolks, remaining 4 eggs and sugar at medium speed for at least 5 minutes or until light and fluffy.
- Melt butter in hot milk.
- Add 1/2 cup flour to egg mixture, beating slowly.
- Add half of hot milk mixture to the egg mixture.
- Add 1 cup flour, then remaining milk. Add remaining flour, vanilla, baking powder and walnuts.
- Pour batter into 3 greased and floured 9-inch cake pans.
- Bake for 20 minutes. Cool slightly before removing from pans.
- Frost with Coconut Frosting and sprinkle with coconut.
- *Note:* A wonderful dessert for a special occasion. Cake layers freeze well.

Coconut Frosting

2 egg whites (reserved from cake ingredients)

1 1/2 cups sugar

5 tablespoons cold water

1/4 teaspoon cream of tartar

2 teaspoons light corn syrup

1 teaspoon vanilla extract

- Place egg whites, sugar, cold water, cream of tartar and corn syrup in top of double boiler and blend well.
- Place over rapidly boiling water and beat constantly until stiff enough to spread, approximately 5 to 7 minutes. Remove from heat and beat in vanilla.

Viennese Hazelnut Cake

Contributed by Jane Martin   **Yield: 12 servings**

7 eggs	1/3 cup bread crumbs
3/4 cup plus 1 tablespoon sugar, divided	1 teaspoon all-purpose flour
	1 1/2 cups heavy cream
1 1/3 cups ground hazelnuts, divided	1 teaspoon vanilla extract

- Preheat oven to 275 degrees.
- Separate 6 eggs. Set aside whites.
- Beat egg yolks and remaining whole egg until thick and pale yellow.
- Beat in 1/2 cup sugar, 1 cup ground hazelnuts and bread crumbs gradually until mixture is thick and dense.
- Beat reserved egg whites in separate bowl until foamy.
- Add 1/4 cup sugar to egg whites 1 tablespoon at a time, beating until stiff peaks form.
- Fold 1/4 of the beaten egg whites into hazelnut mixture.
- Sprinkle flour over batter.
- Fold remaining beaten egg whites into batter thoroughly.
- Butter and flour two 10-inch cake pans and shake off excess flour.
- Pour batter into prepared pans and smooth top with spatula.
- Bake in middle of oven for 35 to 45 minutes or until layers shrink away from sides of pans.
- Cool layers in pans on wire racks, then remove layers from pans.
- Place cooled bottom layer on serving plate.
- Whip heavy cream with 1 tablespoon sugar and vanilla until cream holds its shape firmly.
- Spread 1/4 to 1/3 of the whipped cream on bottom layer.
- Place second layer on top and frost cake with remaining whipped cream.
- Scatter remaining hazelnuts on top and/or sides of cake.
- Serve at once.
- *Note:* Cake layers may be made a day in advance, but do not frost with whipped cream until ready to serve.

Pear Upside-Down Cake

Contributed by Jane Martin

Yield: 6 servings

1/4 cup currant jelly

2 to 3 large pears, peeled, cored and sliced

3/4 cup butter

1 cup sugar

3 eggs

1/2 teaspoon vanilla extract

1/2 teaspoon almond extract

1 1/3 cups all-purpose flour

1/3 cup ground almonds

1 1/2 teaspoons baking powder

Whipped cream to taste

- Preheat oven to 375 degrees.
- Butter 8-inch springform pan and line bottom with waxed paper.
- Spread currant jelly over bottom of pan.
- Arrange pear slices over jelly in concentric circles.
- Cream butter and sugar in large bowl.
- Beat eggs into butter mixture 1 at a time.
- Add vanilla and almond extracts to butter mixture.
- Combine flour, ground almonds and baking powder in separate bowl.
- Add flour mixture to butter mixture gradually, beating thoroughly after each addition.
- Spoon batter over pears and smooth top.
- Bake for 40 minutes.
- Cool in pan for 10 minutes, then invert onto serving plate.
- Serve with whipped cream.
- *Note:* For a festive holiday cake, 1 pound cranberries mixed with 1/2 cup sugar may be substituted for pears.

Plum Cake

Contributed by Jenny Eberhart

Yield: 12 servings

2 cups sugar

1 cup vegetable oil

3 eggs, beaten

2 cups self-rising flour

1 teaspoon ground cloves

1 teaspoon cinnamon

1 cup chopped nuts

2   6-ounce jars plum baby food

1 cup confectioners' sugar

3 tablespoons lemon juice

- Preheat oven to 350 degrees.
- Combine sugar and oil in large bowl. Mix in eggs, flour, cloves, cinnamon, nuts and baby food.
- Pour into greased and floured tube or bundt pan.
- Bake for 1 hour and 10 minutes.
- Cool in pan for 10 minutes. Invert onto serving plate.
- Blend confectioners' sugar and lemon juice. Pour over cake.
- *Note:* May be prepared in 2 small loaf pans, reducing cooking time to 45 minutes. Freezes well.

Greer's Almond Pound Cake

Contributed by Kearsley Walsh

Yield: 12 servings

1 cup butter

3 cups sugar

3 eggs, beaten

3 cups all-purpose flour

1 teaspoon baking powder

1 cup milk

1½ teaspoons almond extract

Confectioners' sugar for dusting

- Preheat oven to 350 degrees.
- Cream butter and sugar. Add eggs 1 at a time, beating for 5 minutes after each addition.
- Add sifted flour and baking powder, milk and almond extract to creamed mixture and mix well.
- Pour into greased and floured bundt pan. Bake for 1 hour.
- Cool and dust with confectioners' sugar.
- *Note:* A deliciously moist pound cake, with the special flavor of almond.

Sour Cream Cake

Contributed by Shirley Shepherd, Maud Mullen

1 cup butter or margarine

2 cups plus 2 teaspoons sugar, divided

2 eggs

8 ounces sour cream

1 teaspoon vanilla extract

2 cups all-purpose flour

1 teaspoon baking powder

1 teaspoon cinnamon

3/4 cup finely chopped pecans

Yield: 12 servings

- Preheat oven to 325 degrees.
- Cream butter and 2 cups sugar. Add eggs and beat well.
- Add sour cream, vanilla, flour and baking powder and mix well.
- Combine remaining sugar, cinnamon and pecans in small bowl.
- Sprinkle half of pecan mixture in bottom of greased tube pan.
- Pour half of batter over pecan mixture.
- Sprinkle remaining pecan mixture over batter layer in tube pan then cover with remaining batter.
- Bake for 1 hour.
- Let cool for 10 minutes in pan, then invert onto serving plate and let cool completely.

Cream Cheese-Chocolate Chip Miniature Cupcakes

Contributed by Sandy King

Yield: 6 dozen

8 ounces cream cheese, softened

1 egg, beaten

1¹/₃ cups sugar, divided

⁵/₈ teaspoon salt, divided

1 cup semisweet miniature chocolate chips

1¹/₂ cups all-purpose flour

¹/₄ cup baking cocoa

1 teaspoon baking soda

1 cup water

¹/₃ cup oil

1 tablespoon vinegar

1 teaspoon vanilla extract

- Preheat oven to 350 degrees.
- Combine cream cheese, egg, ¹/₃ cup sugar and ¹/₈ teaspoon salt and beat well.
- Stir in chocolate chips. Set aside.
- Combine flour, cocoa, ¹/₂ teaspoon salt, 1 cup sugar and baking soda.
- Add water, oil, vinegar and vanilla and mix well.
- Line miniature muffin cups with paper liners or spray with nonstick cooking spray.
- Fill each cup half full with cocoa mixture.
- Top each cup with heaping teaspoon of cream cheese mixture.
- Bake for 20 minutes.

My Great-Grandmother's Spice Cupcakes

Contributed by Emily Dryden

Yield: 12 muffins

1 cup water

1 cup sugar

1 cup raisins

1/2 cup butter

2 cups all-purpose flour

1 teaspoon baking soda

1 teaspoon cinnamon

1/2 teaspoon ground cloves

1/4 teaspoon ground allspice

Pinch of salt

- Preheat oven to 425 degrees.
- Boil water, sugar, raisins and butter together for 3 minutes. Cool.
- Add remaining ingredients to cooled mixture.
- Pour into 12 greased and floured muffin cups.
- Bake for 10 minutes.
- Remove from muffin cups immediately.
- *Note:* These are also nice prepared in 18 miniature muffin cups.

Drop Brownies

Contributed by Diane Paul

Yield: 36 cookies

2 cups chocolate chips

1   14-ounce can sweetened
   condensed milk

½ cup margarine

1 cup all-purpose flour

- Preheat oven to 350 degrees.
- Melt chocolate chips, milk and margarine in saucepan over low heat.
- Stir in flour.
- Drop by rounded teaspoonfuls on ungreased cookie sheet.
- Bake for approximately 7 minutes. Do not overbake, as brownies should be soft.

Chocolate Chip Meringues

Contributed by Margaret McNeily

Yield: 24 servings

4 egg whites

1 cup sugar

¼ teaspoon cream of tartar

½ teaspoon vanilla extract

1 cup chocolate chips

- Preheat oven to 275 degrees.
- Beat egg whites until stiff but not dry.
- Sift in sugar and cream of tartar slowly.
- Add vanilla and fold in chocolate chips.
- Drop by large tablespoonfuls onto waxed paper-covered cookie sheet.
- Bake for 30 minutes.
- Cool slightly before removing with spatula.
- *Note:* Kids love them.

Chocolate Chip Pizza

Contributed by Lee Ann Dean

Yield: 15 servings

1 roll refrigerated chocolate chip cookie dough, softened

8 ounces cream cheese, softened

⅓ cup sugar

Mini-chocolate chips, coconut and chocolate jimmies to taste

- Preheat oven to 375 degrees.
- Press softened cookie dough onto pizza pan.
- Bake for 10 to 12 minutes until dough is golden brown. Do not overbake. Let cool.
- Mix cream cheese and sugar.
- Spread cream cheese mixture onto cooled cookie dough.
- Top with mini-chocolate chips, coconut and jimmies.
- *Note:* Fresh fruit pizza is a great variation. To prepare, follow instructions above using sugar cookie dough (in place of chocolate chip cookie dough) and fresh fruit for toppings.

Chocolate Rum Balls

Contributed by Connie Greendoner

Yield: 48 balls

1 cup semisweet chocolate chips

½ cup sugar

⅓ cup rum

3 tablespoons light corn syrup

2 cups crushed vanilla wafers

1 cup ground walnuts

Confectioners' sugar

- Melt chocolate chips in saucepan over low heat.
- Remove saucepan from heat and stir in sugar, rum and corn syrup.
- Fold vanilla wafers and walnuts into chocolate mixture.
- Form mixture into 1-inch balls, using 2 teaspoons of mixture for each ball.
- Roll balls in confectioners' sugar.
- Store in airtight container.

Chewy Cheesecake Cookies

Contributed by Diane Wood

Yield: 24 cookies

½ cup butter, softened

3 ounces cream cheese, softened

1 cup sugar

1 cup all-purpose flour

½ cup chopped pecans

- Preheat oven to 350 degrees.
- Cream together butter and cream cheese.
- Add sugar gradually, beating until light and fluffy.
- Add flour and beat well.
- Stir in pecans.
- Shape dough into 1-inch balls.
- Place balls 2 inches apart on ungreased cookie sheet.
- Dip bottom of a glass in water and press each cookie gently until 2 inches in diameter.
- Bake for 8 to 10 minutes. Do not brown.
- Cool on cookie sheet for 1 minute, then remove promptly to prevent sticking.
- *Note:* These cookies are hard when cooled, but are still chewy.

Chocolate Cracks

Contributed by Martha White

Yield: 72 cookies

3 cups all-purpose flour

1¼ teaspoons baking soda

½ teaspoon salt

1½ cups packed dark brown sugar

¾ cup butter

2 tablespoons water

2 cups semisweet chocolate chips

2 eggs

- Preheat oven to 350 degrees.
- Sift together flour, baking soda and salt. Set aside.
- Combine brown sugar, butter and water in large saucepan and heat until butter melts, stirring constantly.
- Add chocolate chips and stir until chocolate is thoroughly melted.
- Cool chocolate mixture for 5 minutes.
- Beat eggs into chocolate mixture 1 at a time.
- Add flour mixture and blend well.
- Let dough stand for approximately 10 minutes or until it can be handled easily.
- Roll dough into balls using 1 teaspoon of dough for each ball.
- Place balls on aluminum foil-lined cookie sheet.
- Bake for 9 minutes.
- Let cookies cool on foil for 10 minutes, and then remove from cookie sheet with spatula. Cookies should be chewy when cool.

Cookie "Wow!"

Contributed by Jane Kipp

Yield: 112 large cookies

2 cups butter

2 cups sugar

2 cups packed brown sugar

4 eggs

2 teaspoons vanilla extract

5 cups oats

4 cups all-purpose flour

1 tablespoon salt

2 tablespoons baking powder

2 tablespoons baking soda

4 cups semisweet chocolate chips

1 8-ounce chocolate candy bar, grated (optional)

3 cups chopped nuts

- Preheat oven to 375 degrees.
- Cream butter with sugar and brown sugar.
- Add eggs and vanilla to creamed mixture and beat well.
- Grind oats in blender until powdery.
- Stir flour, oats, salt, baking powder and baking soda into batter gradually.
- Add chocolate chips, grated chocolate and nuts to batter.
- Form batter into golf ball-sized balls and place 2 inches apart on ungreased cookie sheet. Bake for 15 minutes.

Gingerbread Cookies

Contributed by Karen Lazar

Yield: 48 cookies

½ cup butter

1 cup sugar

1 cup packed brown sugar

1 cup dark molasses

1 cup all-purpose flour

2 teaspoons baking soda

½ teaspoon ground cloves

1 teaspoon cinnamon

2 teaspoons ginger

1 teaspoon salt

¼ cup water

2 egg whites

3 cups confectioners' sugar

Food coloring

- Preheat oven to 350 degrees.
- Cream butter, sugar and brown sugar.
- Add molasses and beat well.
- Sift together flour, baking soda, cloves, cinnamon, ginger and salt.
- Add to creamed mixture ⅓ at a time, alternately with water, mixing well after each addition.
- Roll out dough on lightly floured surface.
- Cut with cookie cutters.
- Bake on lightly greased cookie sheet for 8 minutes or until cookies spring back when pressed with finger. Let cool.
- Combine egg whites and confectioners' sugar.
- Add water until icing reaches desired consistency.
- Divide icing into small bowls and add food coloring as desired.
- Use small paintbrush to apply icing to cooled cookies.
- *Note:* This icing hardens and is not messy when eaten.

Linzer Tarts

Contributed by
Beverley Brainard Fleming

1 cup butter, softened

1½ cups sugar

1 egg

1½ teaspoons vanilla extract

3½ cups all-purpose flour

1 teaspoon salt

½ to ¾ cups red raspberry
  preserves

Confectioners' sugar to taste

½ cup ground hazelnuts
  (optional)

Yield: 50 cookies

- Cream butter and sugar in large bowl until light and fluffy.
- Add egg and vanilla and beat well.
- Blend in flour and salt to form a smooth dough, mixing with hands if necessary.
- Refrigerate dough for 2 hours.
- Preheat oven to 375 degrees.
- Roll out half the dough to ⅛-inch thickness on floured board.
- Cut with 2½-inch round cookie cutter.
- Roll out remaining dough and cut with 2½-inch round cookie cutter with 1-inch hole in the center.
- Bake cookies on lightly greased cookie sheets for 8 to 10 minutes or until lightly browned.
- Cool cookies for 30 minutes.
- Spread raspberry preserves on whole cookies and top with cut-out cookies.
- Sprinkle with confectioners' sugar and hazelnuts.

Lace Cookies

Contributed by Mary Lu Pamm

Yield: 3 dozen

1 cup oats

1 cup sugar

3 tablespoons all-purpose flour

1/2 teaspoon salt

1/2 teaspoon baking powder

1/2 teaspoon vanilla extract

1/2 cup butter, melted

1 egg, beaten

- Preheat oven to 350 degrees.
- Combine dry ingredients in large bowl. Add vanilla and butter and mix well.
- Add egg and stir to combine.
- Drop by scant 1/2 teaspoonfuls onto foil-lined cookie sheet.
- Bake for 7 minutes.
- Let cool and peel cookies off foil.
- *Note:* Cookies may be rolled up or shaped into cups while warm and filled with whipped cream, custard or fruit when cool.

Pecan Sandies

Contributed by Diane Wood

Yield: 50 cookies

1 cup butter or margarine, softened

1/3 cup sugar

2 teaspoons water

2 teaspoons vanilla extract

2 cups all-purpose flour

1 cup chopped pecans

Confectioners' sugar

- Cream butter and sugar in large bowl. Add water and vanilla and mix well.
- Mix in flour and pecans.
- Chill for 4 hours.
- Preheat oven to 325 degrees.
- Shape dough into 1-inch balls.
- Bake on ungreased cookie sheet for 20 minutes.
- Remove from sheet, cool slightly, and roll in confectioners' sugar.
- *Note:* Walnuts may be substituted for pecans.

Lemon Squares

Contributed by
Nancy Haigh

2 cups plus 6 tablespoons
all-purpose flour, divided

Pinch of salt

1/2 cup confectioners' sugar

1 cup butter or margarine

2 cups sugar

4 eggs

Juice of 2 lemons

Grated rind of 1 lemon

Yield: 16 servings

▪ Preheat oven to 350 degrees.

▪ Combine 2 cups flour, salt and confectioners' sugar.

▪ Cut butter into flour mixture with pastry blender or 2 knives until mixture is crumbly.

▪ Pat mixture evenly into 9x13-inch baking pan.

▪ Bake for 20 minutes, remove from oven, and set aside.

▪ Combine remaining flour, sugar, eggs, lemon juice and lemon rind and mix well.

▪ Pour lemon mixture over baked crust.

▪ Return pan to oven and bake for 20 minutes more or until set. Let cool.

▪ Dust with additional confectioners' sugar.

▪ Cut into squares.

▪ *Note:* May be frozen.

Orange Sugar Cookies

Contributed by Marilyn Hayward

Yield: 72 cookies

2/3 cup unsalted butter, softened

1½ cups sugar

2 eggs

3 cups all-purpose flour

1½ teaspoons salt

2 teaspoons baking powder

1 tablespoon orange juice

Grated rind of 1 orange

- Preheat oven to 350 degrees.
- Cream butter and sugar until fluffy.
- Add eggs and beat well.
- Sift flour, salt and baking powder together and add gradually to butter mixture.
- Stir in orange juice and orange rind.
- Wrap dough tightly and chill until firm.
- Roll out dough thinly on floured surface and cut into desired shapes.
- Bake on greased cookie sheets for approximately 8 to 10 minutes, or until just beginning to brown around edges.

Chocolate Peppermint Bars

Contributed by Kathy Pankowski

Yield: 4 dozen

4 ounces semisweet chocolate, melted

1½ cups plus 2 tablespoons butter, softened and divided

4 eggs

2 cups sugar

1 cup all-purpose flour

2 cups confectioners' sugar

1 tablespoon cream

1 teaspoon peppermint extract

¾ cup chocolate chips

- Preheat oven to 350 degrees.
- Combine melted chocolate and 1 cup butter and stir until well blended.
- Beat in eggs 1 at a time.
- Add sugar and flour and blend well.
- Spread batter into greased and floured 11x15-inch jelly roll pan.
- Bake for 20 to 25 minutes and then cool completely.
- Combine confectioners' sugar, 6 tablespoons butter, cream and peppermint extract.
- Spread over cooled cake layer and chill.
- Melt chocolate chips with 4 tablespoons butter.
- Spread over chilled layer.
- Cut into bars.

Scotcheroos

Contributed by Beth Ann Wahl

Yield: 12 servings

½ cup sugar
½ cup corn syrup
½ cup peanut butter
3 cups Rice Krispies
½ cup chocolate chips
½ cup butterscotch chips

- Combine sugar and corn syrup in large saucepan and heat to boiling.
- Remove saucepan from heat and add peanut butter, stirring until smooth.
- Add Rice Krispies to saucepan and stir until well coated.
- Press Rice Krispies mixture into greased 9-inch square pan.
- Melt chocolate and butterscotch chips in small double boiler or microwave.
- Spread melted mixture over Rice Krispies mixture.
- Let harden.
- Cut into squares and serve.

Walnut Refrigerator Cookies

Contributed by Diane Wood

Yield: 6 dozen

1³/₄ cups walnuts, divided

2 cups all-purpose flour

1 cup margarine, softened

¹/₂ cup sugar

¹/₂ cup packed brown sugar

1 teaspoon vanilla extract

¹/₄ teaspoon salt

¹/₄ teaspoon baking soda

1 egg

- Chop 1 cup walnuts and reserve remaining walnuts.
- Beat remaining ingredients in mixer bowl at low speed until blended.
- Stir in chopped walnuts.
- Shape dough into three 5-inch long rolls with floured hands.
- Wrap rolls in waxed paper and refrigerate for 2 hours or until firm enough to slice.
- Preheat oven to 350 degrees.
- Slice one roll of dough into ¹/₄-inch slices.
- Place slices 1 inch apart on greased cookie sheet and press a reserved walnut on top of each slice.
- Bake for 8 to 10 minutes or until lightly browned.
- Cool cookies on wire rack.
- Repeat with remaining dough rolls.
- Store cookies in tightly covered container for up to 2 weeks.
- *Note:* Dough can be refrigerated for up to 1 week before baking.

Brandy Alexander Pie

Contributed by Phyllis DeMaio

Yield: 8 servings

1 tablespoon unflavored gelatin

½ cup cold water

⅔ cup sugar, divided

⅛ teaspoon salt

3 eggs, separated

¼ cup Cognac

¼ cup Crème de Cacao

1 cup heavy cream

1 9-inch chocolate wafer pie shell, chilled

- Sprinkle gelatin over cold water in saucepan.
- Add ⅓ cup sugar, salt and egg yolks to gelatin mixture.
- Heat mixture over low heat until gelatin dissolves and mixture thickens, but do not boil.
- Remove saucepan from heat and stir in Cognac and Crème de Cacao.
- Place saucepan in refrigerator and chill until mixture begins to thicken and mound when stirred.
- Beat egg whites in separate bowl until firm.
- Add remaining sugar to egg whites and continue beating until stiff.
- Fold egg whites into thickened liqueur mixture gently.
- Whip cream in separate bowl until thickened, but not stiff.
- Fold whipped cream into liqueur mixture to make pie filling.
- Turn pie filling gently into chilled shell.
- Chill for at least 3 hours.
- *Note:* Garnish with chocolate curls and additional whipped cream for an elegant dessert.

Frozen Citrus Pie

Contributed by Jentje Cain

Yield: 6 servings

1   6-ounce can frozen
lemonade or limeade
concentrate, thawed

1   8-ounce package frozen
whipped topping, softened

1 pint vanilla ice cream,
softened

1   9-inch graham cracker pie
shell

- Combine lemonade, whipped topping and ice cream.
- Pour mixture into graham cracker shell.
- Freeze.
- *Note:* A refreshing and simple summer dessert.

Chocolate-Pecan Pie

Contributed by Mary Rice

Yield: 12 servings

2 ounces unsweetened
chocolate

1/4 cup butter

4 eggs

3/4 cup sugar

1 1/4 cups dark corn syrup

1 1/2 teaspoons vanilla extract

3 tablespoons rum

2 cups pecan halves

1   10-inch unbaked pie shell

- Preheat oven to 350 degrees.
- Melt chocolate and butter in top of double boiler. Cool slightly.
- Combine eggs, sugar and corn syrup in large bowl.
- Add vanilla, rum and chocolate mixture to egg mixture and mix well. Stir in pecans and pour mixture into pie shell.
- Bake for 50 minutes or until top is soft, but middle still moves slightly when shaken.
- Remove pie from oven and cool on rack to room temperature.
- *Note:* This pie is rich, rich, rich.

Fresh Fruit Pie

Contributed by Lee Wakefield

Yield: 6 servings

¼ cup margarine, softened

¾ cup sugar, divided

1 egg yolk

1 cup all-purpose flour

3 tablespoons cornstarch

1½ cups orange juice

¼ cup lemon juice

1 teaspoon grated lemon rind

6 cups cut-up fresh fruit

- Preheat oven to 400 degrees.
- Combine margarine, ¼ cup sugar and egg yolk and mix well.
- Add flour gradually.
- Press mixture into 9-inch pie plate.
- Bake for 8 minutes, remove from oven and let cool.
- Blend remaining sugar and cornstarch in saucepan.
- Add orange juice.
- Bring mixture to a boil, stirring constantly. Boil for 1 minute.
- Add lemon juice and rind to orange mixture. Cool.
- Fold fruit into cooled mixture and turn into cooled crust.
- Chill pie in refrigerator for at least 4 hours before serving.
- *Note:* Use any fruit in season, such as melon, grapes, berries, peaches, plums or apricots, for this wonderful summertime fare. Cannot be frozen.

Pumpkin Chiffon Pie

Contributed by Jane Martin

Yield: 8 servings

2 cups vanilla wafer crumbs

6 tablespoons butter, melted and cooled

3/4 cup plus 1/3 cup sugar, divided

1/2 cup coarsely chopped pecans

4 teaspoons unflavored gelatin

1/4 cup Drambuie

1 1/2 cups pumpkin purée

1/2 cup heavy cream

3/4 teaspoon cinnamon

1/2 teaspoon ginger

1/2 teaspoon nutmeg

1/4 teaspoon allspice

1/4 teaspoon salt

3 egg yolks

4 egg whites

Pinch of cream of tartar

- Preheat oven to 400 degrees.
- Combine vanilla wafer crumbs, melted butter, 1/4 cup sugar and pecans and pat onto bottom and sides of 10-inch tart dish to form pie shell.
- Bake for 10 minutes and cool on rack.
- Sprinkle gelatin over Drambuie and let stand for 5 minutes.
- Stir gelatin mixture over hot water until gelatin is dissolved.
- Combine pumpkin purée, heavy cream, 1/2 cup sugar, cinnamon, ginger, nutmeg, allspice, salt and egg yolks in large saucepan.
- Cook mixture over low heat for 10 minutes, stirring constantly.
- Stir gelatin mixture into pumpkin mixture, transfer to large bowl and set aside to cool.
- Beat egg whites with cream of tartar until soft peaks form.
- Add remaining 1/3 cup sugar, 2 tablespoons at a time, beating until stiff peaks form.
- Fold beaten egg whites into cooled pumpkin mixture.
- Pour mixture into pie shell.
- Chill, covered, for at least 6 hours.
- *Note:* A Thanksgiving tradition.

Baklava

Contributed by Carla Stone Bassett

Yield: 12 servings

5½ cups all-purpose flour

1 teaspoon salt (optional)

1 cup butter, melted

2 cups crushed walnuts

2 teaspoons cinnamon

4 cups water

4 cups sugar

½ teaspoon vanilla extract

- Preheat oven to 350 degrees.
- Combine flour and salt in a large bowl with enough lukewarm water to make a stiff dough. Knead briefly.
- Divide dough into 10 small balls and roll into very thin sheets. Let stand to dry.
- Lay 1 sheet of dough on lightly buttered cookie sheet, sprinkle with melted butter and lay another sheet of dough on top, repeating until half of dough is used.
- Combine walnuts and cinnamon and spread over dough layers.
- Continue to layer remaining dough and melted butter as above.
- Cut into diamond-shaped serving-sized pieces.
- Bake for 20 to 25 minutes or until top layers are crisp.
- Boil 4 cups water, sugar and vanilla in saucepan until sugar is melted into a syrup.
- Pour mixture over baklava while still hot. Cool and serve cold.
- *Note:* Purchased phyllo dough may be used instead of homemade dough, but if substitution is made, sprinkle butter over every other sheet rather than over each sheet.

Prize Winning Pumpkin Cheesecake

Contributed by
Beverley Brainard Fleming

Yield: 12 servings

3 cups finely ground
  gingersnaps

1/2 cup confectioners' sugar

3/4 cup butter, melted

2 8-ounce packages cream
   cheese, softened

5 eggs

3/4 cup packed light brown
  sugar

1 16-ounce can solid-pack
   pumpkin

1 1/2 teaspoons cinnamon

1/4 teaspoon ground cloves

1/4 teaspoon ginger

1/4 teaspoon mace

1/4 teaspoon nutmeg

1 teaspoon vanilla extract

1/2 cup Brandy, divided

2 cups sour cream

1/4 cup sugar

- Preheat oven to 350 degrees.
- Combine gingersnap crumbs, confectioners' sugar and melted butter.
- Press crumb mixture onto bottom and side of 9-inch ungreased springform pan.
- Beat cream cheese with electric mixer on medium speed.
- Add eggs, brown sugar, pumpkin, spices, vanilla and 1/4 cup Brandy to cream cheese and mix until smooth.
- Pour pumpkin mixture into prepared pan and bake for 40 minutes or until edge of cheesecake begins to pull away from side of pan.
- Remove cheesecake from oven and reset oven to 400 degrees.
- Whisk together sour cream, sugar and remaining Brandy in small bowl.
- Spread sour cream mixture over baked cheesecake, return to oven and bake for 10 minutes more.
- Chill cheesecake overnight.
- *Note:* This recipe won a prize in Creative Cooking's cheesecake contest. Best when prepared 2 days in advance of serving.

Toffee Tart

Contributed by Julie Lowe

Yield: 12 servings

2 cups all-purpose flour

1/2 cup sugar

10 tablespoons unsalted
butter, chilled, chopped

4 egg yolks, divided

3¼ cups plus 2 tablespoons
heavy cream, divided

2 eggs

2¼ cups Caramel Sauce,
divided (recipe on page 225)

6 ounces semisweet chocolate

Chocolate Ganache (recipe on
page 225)

Chocolate bar

- Combine flour and sugar in bowl of food processor.
- Add butter and process until mixture is consistency of cornmeal.
- Beat 1 egg yolk with 1 tablespoon heavy cream. Add to flour mixture and pulse until dough forms, adding up to 1 tablespoon more cream if needed. Form dough into ball, wrap in plastic wrap and chill for 1 to 2 hours.
- Preheat oven to 375 degrees.
- Roll dough into large circle and fit into loose-bottomed tart pan, trimming edges. Line shell with foil or parchment and fill with dried beans or uncooked rice.
- Bake for 5 to 10 minutes or until edges are lightly browned.
- Remove from oven and reduce oven temperature to 350 degrees. Remove beans and foil.
- Whisk together 1¾ cups heavy cream, remaining 3 egg yolks, eggs and 1½ cups Caramel Sauce to make toffee filling.
- Melt chocolate and paint inside of warm crust with chocolate.
- Pour toffee filling into crust and bake for 45 to 60 minutes or until set. Let cool and chill for at least 4 hours.
- Spread Chocolate Ganache over tart and chill for 1 hour more.
- Set aside a small amount of Caramel Sauce and whip remaining cream and remaining Caramel Sauce together until stiff to make topping.
- Scrape edge of chocolate bar with vegetable peeler to make chocolate shavings.
- Spread topping over chilled tart or decorate with pastry bag fitted with star tip. Drizzle with remaining Caramel Sauce and top with chocolate shavings.
- Chill tart until ready to serve.
- *Note:* A spectacular dessert.

Caramel Sauce

2 cups sugar

2 tablespoons freshly
squeezed lemon juice

1/2 cup unsalted butter

1¾ cups heavy cream

■ Heat sugar and lemon juice in
heavy saucepan over medium
heat, stirring constantly until
sugar turns dark brown.

■ Remove saucepan from heat and
stir in butter until melted.

■ Stir in cream and mix until
sauce is smooth. Mixture may
break up at first, but will
reincorporate with mixing.

■ Set aside at room temperature.

Chocolate Ganache

4 ounces semisweet chocolate,
chopped

2 ounces bitter chocolate,
chopped

2 ounces milk chocolate,
chopped

1/2 cup heavy cream

1 tablespoon unsalted butter

■ Place chocolate in bowl.

■ Heat cream to just below boiling
and pour over chocolate. Whisk
until smooth. Place bowl over
boiling water and continue to
whisk if chocolate does not melt
completely.

■ Stir in butter and whisk until
smooth.

Cranberry-Walnut Tart

Contributed by Jane Martin

Yield: 8 servings

1⅓ cups all-purpose flour

2 tablespoons sugar

¾ teaspoon salt, divided

½ cup cold unsalted butter, cut into bits

1 egg yolk beaten with 1½ tablespoons ice water

3 eggs

⅔ cup packed dark brown sugar

⅔ cup light corn syrup

½ cup unsalted butter, melted and cooled

1 teaspoon vanilla extract

1¼ cups chopped cranberries

1 cup chopped walnuts or pecans

- Combine flour, sugar and ¼ teaspoon salt in large bowl.
- Add cold butter and blend with pastry blender until mixture resembles coarse cornmeal.
- Add yolk mixture and blend until moisture is absorbed.
- Form dough into ball.
- Dust dough ball with additional flour and chill, covered, for 1 hour.
- Roll out dough on floured surface until ⅛ inch thick.
- Place dough in 10-inch tart pan with removable fluted rim.
- Chill for 30 minutes.
- Preheat oven to 425 degrees.
- Cover dough with foil and weight with uncooked rice.
- Bake for 15 minutes, then remove foil and rice.
- Bake for 5 to 10 minutes more or until pale golden brown.
- Cool on rack.
- Reset oven to 350 degrees.
- Combine eggs, brown sugar, corn syrup, melted butter, remaining ½ teaspoon salt and vanilla and whisk until smooth.
- Add cranberries and walnuts and stir.
- Pour mixture into cooled shell.
- Bake for 40 to 45 minutes or until golden brown.
- Cool completely on rack.
- Remove rim of pan and slide tart onto serving dish.
- *Note:* This may be prepared a day in advance and stored, covered, at room temperature.

Chocolate Mousse

Contributed by Jane Martin

Yield: 8 servings

1 cup chocolate chips

2 eggs, separated

1 tablespoon strong coffee

1 cup heavy cream

½ tablespoon superfine sugar

1 teaspoon vanilla extract

Sweetened whipped cream to taste for garnish

- Melt chocolate chips in double boiler.
- Beat egg yolks lightly.
- Beat coffee and beaten egg yolks into melted chocolate and set aside.
- Beat egg whites in separate bowl until stiff. Set aside.
- Combine heavy cream, sugar and vanilla in separate bowl and beat until whipped.
- Fold egg whites into chocolate mixture.
- Fold whipped cream into chocolate mixture.
- Pour into serving bowl and refrigerate.
- Serve with sweetened whipped cream.
- *Note:* For a large crowd, quadruple and serve in a pretty crystal bowl. For a delicious variation, substitute 1 tablespoon orange juice and 1 teaspoon grated orange rind for the coffee and vanilla extract.

Lemon Mousse

Contributed by Sharon Larrimer

Yield: 6 servings

2 lemons

1 tablespoon unflavored gelatin

4 eggs, separated

¼ cup sugar

1 cup heavy cream, divided

¼ cup slivered almonds, toasted

- Grate lemon rind and set aside.
- Squeeze juice from lemons into large saucepan.
- Sprinkle gelatin over lemon juice and let stand for 10 minutes.
- Combine egg yolks, grated lemon rind and sugar in small bowl and beat until light and lemon-colored.
- Heat gelatin mixture and stir to dissolve. Remove saucepan from heat.
- Stir a small amount of hot gelatin mixture into egg mixture, then stir egg mixture into hot gelatin.
- Whip ¾ cup cream in chilled bowl until thick but not stiff.
- Beat egg whites until stiff but not dry.
- Fold whipped cream, then egg whites, into egg mixture gently. Pour mixture into 2-quart serving dish or individual parfait glasses.
- Chill.
- Whip remaining cream just before serving. Garnish mousse with whipped cream and almonds.
- *Note:* A refreshing, light-tasting dessert, especially good after a heavy meal.

Lethal Chocolate Terrine

Contributed by John M. Sablian,
Chef-Mt. Cuba; courtesy of
Mrs. Lammot duPont Copeland

Yield: 10 servings

6 ounces semisweet chocolate	2 eggs
3 cups heavy cream or 1¹/₂ pints	Vanilla Sauce (recipe follows)
¹/₄ cup dark rum	1 pint fresh raspberries, puréed and strained

- Melt chocolate in double boiler and set aside.
- Beat heavy cream until whipped and refrigerate.
- Combine rum and eggs in separate double boiler and beat over low heat until foamy and heated through. Remove from heat.
- Fold chocolate into egg mixture and transfer to large bowl.
- Fold whipped cream into chocolate mixture. Pour mixture into waxed paper-lined 4x10-inch loaf or terrine pan.
- Refrigerate for at least 6 hours to overnight and freeze for 2 hours before serving.
- Pour Vanilla Sauce onto individual serving plates.
- Place slice of terrine over top.
- Drizzle puréed raspberries onto sauce and run toothpick through raspberries and sauce to form pattern.
- Serve immediately.

Vanilla Sauce

3 eggs	1 whole fresh vanilla bean
¹/₂ cup sugar	1¹/₂ cups heavy cream

- Combine eggs and sugar in double boiler with wire whisk.
- Cut vanilla bean into halves lengthwise and scrape into egg mixture.
- Heat cream until warm and stir into egg mixture.
- Heat, whisking until foamy; do not boil. Remove from heat. Refrigerate for at least 2 hours.
- *Note:* May substitute ¹/₂ teaspoon vanilla extract for vanilla bean.

Desserts ▪ Sweets

See also...

- Bailey's Irish Cream-Chocolate Chip Cheesecake
- Banana-Pecan Bread Pudding with Praline Whiskey Sauce
- Chocolate-Almond Meringues
- Chocolate-Peanut Butter Pie
- Heath Bar Cheesecake
- The Hotel duPont's Famous Almond Macaroons

...in the Restaurant Section

Restaurants

Nemours

Spend a day in Europe amid the grandeur of the Nemours Mansion and Gardens. Erected by Alfred I. du Pont, this 102-room glittering French château stands among 300 acres of gardens, statuary and lush woodlands.

Stuffed Mushrooms à la Grècque

*Contributed by The Longwood Inn,
Kennett Square, Pennsylvania,
the mushroom capital of the world*

36 large mushrooms, stems
removed

1 pound lean bacon, finely
chopped

½ pound ham, finely chopped

4 cups seasoned croutons,
ground

1 pound feta cheese, half
grated and half sliced thinly

1½ cups grated Romano
cheese

1 pound ripe tomatoes,
peeled, seeded and chopped

Yield: 36 hors d'oeuvres

- Preheat oven to 350 degrees.
- Steam or blanch mushroom caps until tender, approximately 1½ minutes, and let cool.
- Combine chopped bacon, chopped ham, ground croutons, grated feta cheese and Romano cheese in mixing bowl to make filling.
- Add chopped tomatoes to filling and mix thoroughly.
- Stuff each mushroom cap with about 2 ounces of filling.
- Top each mushroom cap with small slice of feta cheese.
- Bake, uncovered, for 12 to 15 minutes.
- *Note:* If filling falls apart, add more ground seasoned croutons.

Shiitake and Smoked Salmon Canapés

Contributed by Longwood Inn,
Kennett Square, Pennsylvania,
the mushroom capital of the world

3 tablespoons plus ¼ cup
  butter, divided

3 cups sliced fresh shiitake
  mushrooms, about 8 ounces

2 tablespoons chopped shallots

1 tablespoon soy sauce

2 cups heavy cream

1½ pounds cream cheese,
  room temperature

8 ounces jumbo lump crab
  meat

120 bread rounds, plain or
  toasted, or cucumber slices

½ pound smoked salmon,
  thinly sliced

3 tablespoons chopped fresh
  dill

Yield: 120 canapés

- Heat 3 tablespoons butter in large skillet.

- Stir in mushrooms, shallots and soy sauce and sauté over medium heat until mushrooms become soft.

- Add heavy cream to skillet and simmer until reduced by half.

- Remove skillet from heat and let mushroom mixture cool.

- Beat cream cheese in mixing bowl until smooth.

- Fold in crab meat and sautéed mushroom mixture.

- Refrigerate for 1 hour.

- Remove remaining butter from refrigerator and allow to soften.

- Spread bread or cucumber rounds with softened butter and top with ½ tablespoon of mixture.

- Wrap or top canapés with smoked salmon and sprinkle with dill.

- *Note:* Grated cucumber or tiny honey mushrooms may be used to garnish canapés.

Fresh Salsa

*Contributed by The University and
Whist Club, Wilmington, Delaware*

Yield: 3 cups

2 to 3 cloves of garlic

1/4 cup fresh parsley leaves

1/2 cup fresh cilantro

1 jalapeño pepper, seeded

2 to 3 vine-ripened summer
  tomatoes, diced

1 medium-sized yellow onion,
  diced

1 4-ounce can green chilies,
  chopped and drained

3 tablespoons red wine vinegar

1 tablespoon oregano

1/2 teaspoon pepper

3 tablespoons olive oil

- Mince together garlic, parsley, cilantro and jalapeño pepper.
- Combine minced herb mixture and remaining ingredients in large bowl and mix well.
- Refrigerate overnight before serving.

- *Note:* Serve with tortilla chips or use with fajitas. If vine-ripened summer tomatoes are not available, 3 to 4 regular tomatoes can be substituted.

Hot Crab Dip

*Contributed by The Corner Cupboard
Inn, Rehoboth Beach, Delaware*

Yield: 4 cups

24 ounces cream cheese

1 pound fresh or
  2 7-ounce cans crab meat

1/2 cup mayonnaise

2 tablespoons mustard

1 tablespoon horseradish

1 teaspoon onion juice

Salt and pepper to taste

1/2 cup Sherry

- Combine all ingredients except Sherry in top of double boiler and heat until creamy.

- Add Sherry and stir.
- Serve in chafing dish.

Lobster and Corn Chowder

Contributed by The Back Burner,
Hockessin, Delaware

Yield: 6 servings

4 ounces bacon, chopped

1 small onion, chopped

1 small green bell pepper, chopped

⅓ cup all-purpose flour

4 cups milk

1 cup heavy cream

4 ears of corn, shucked, or 9 ounces frozen corn

Nutmeg, mace and cayenne pepper to taste

¼ cup butter

Salt and white pepper to taste

1 pound (2 cups) shelled, cooked lobster meat or lobster tails

- Fry bacon until crisp in large stockpot or heavy kettle. Remove bacon from pot and drain on paper towels.
- Remove most of bacon fat from pot and return bacon to pot.
- Add onion and green pepper, and sauté for 5 minutes.
- Add flour to pot and blend well.
- Add milk and cream to pot gradually, stirring constantly.
- Stir over medium-high heat until soup thickens, approximately 10 to 15 minutes.
- Cut kernels from corn ears with sharp knife and add to soup.
- Stir in nutmeg, mace, cayenne pepper and butter.
- Season soup with salt and white pepper.
- Add lobster to soup and simmer for 5 minutes.

Crab and Corn Bisque

Contributed by The Back Burner,
Hockessin, Delaware

¹/₂ cup butter

1¹/₂ cups chopped green onion
tops

2 tablespoons all-purpose
flour

1¹/₂ tablespoons Creole
seafood seasoning

1 teaspoon granulated garlic

Thyme to taste

4 cups Crab Stock (recipe
follows)

2   12-ounce cans whole
kernel corn, drained

1¹/₂ cups heavy cream

1 pound lump crab meat

Yield: 8 servings

- Melt butter in 3-quart saucepan over medium heat. Add onion tops, and sauté until wilted.
- Stir in flour and seasonings. Continue cooking until flour begins to stick to pan, stirring constantly. Blend in Crab Stock, reduce heat and simmer for 15 minutes or until stock thickens, stirring constantly.
- Add corn and simmer for 15 minutes more. Stir in cream slowly.
- Add crab meat and mix gently.
- Remove saucepan from heat and let stand for 30 minutes.
- Reheat over very low heat, stirring gently so crab meat does not flake and cream does not curdle. Do not boil. Serve immediately.

Crab Stock

6 cups water

6 hard-shelled medium-sized
crabs

6 stalks celery

2 medium-sized onions,
quartered

1¹/₂ tablespoons liquid crab
boil (optional)

Yield: 1 quart

- Combine all ingredients in large saucepan and bring to a boil over high heat.
- Reduce heat and simmer for 3 hours, adding more water as needed to make 1 quart of stock.
- Strain.

Chilled Shrimp and Cucumber Soup

Contributed by The Back Burner,
Hockessin, Delaware

Yield: 6 servings

2 large cucumbers, peeled, seeded and coarsely chopped

1/4 cup red wine vinegar

1 tablespoon sugar

1 teaspoon salt

1 pound small raw shrimp, peeled and deveined

2 tablespoons unsalted butter

1/4 cup dry white vermouth

Salt to taste

Freshly ground black pepper to taste

1 1/2 cups buttermilk, chilled

3/4 cup chopped fresh dill

Sprigs of fresh dill for garnish

- Toss cucumbers with vinegar, sugar and salt and let stand for 30 minutes.
- Rinse shrimp and pat dry.
- Melt butter in small skillet, add shrimp and toss over medium-high heat until pink, about 2 to 3 minutes.
- Remove shrimp from skillet with slotted spoon and set aside in small bowl.
- Add vermouth to skillet and boil until reduced to a few spoonfuls.
- Pour reduced vermouth over shrimp and season with salt and pepper.
- Drain cucumbers and transfer to food processor fitted with steel blade.
- Process cucumbers briefly, add buttermilk and continue to process until smooth. Add dill and pulse once.
- Pour cucumber mixture into large bowl, add shrimp mixture and refrigerate, covered, until very cold.
- Serve in chilled bowls, garnished with sprigs of fresh dill.
- *Note:* Other fresh herbs, such as parsley or mint, can be substituted for dill.

Chicken Salad with Basil-Lime Vinaigrette

Contributed by The Urban Picnic,
Wilmington, Delaware

Yield: 4 servings

2 whole chicken breasts, halved

1 small head radicchio, torn into bite-sized pieces

1 head Belgian endive, cut into bite-sized pieces

1 bunch maché or lamb lettuce, roots trimmed

1 carrot, peeled and grated or julienned

Basil-Lime Vinaigrette (recipe follows)

- Poach chicken, cool, remove skin and bones and cut into bite-sized pieces.

- Toss chicken and vegetables together in large bowl.

- Just before serving, toss in just enough Basil-Lime Vinaigrette to coat well.

- *Note:* To poach chicken, lay breasts in single layer in roasting pan with a little water, wedge of yellow onion, celery stalk and chunks of carrot. Cover tightly with lid or foil and bake at 350 degrees for 20 to 25 minutes.

Basil-Lime Vinaigrette

3 tablespoons freshly squeezed lime juice

1/4 cup vegetable oil or walnut oil

1/4 teaspoon salt

1/2 teaspoon freshly ground black pepper

1 clove of garlic, minced

1 teaspoon coriander

3 tablespoons each minced fresh basil and fresh parsley

Sugar to taste

Crushed red pepper flakes to taste

- Combine all ingredients and refrigerate.

Dijon-Hoisin Crusted Pork Tenderloin with Three-Pepper Marmalade

Contributed by La La Land Restaurant, Rehoboth Beach, Delaware

Yield: 10 servings

3/4 cup Dijon mustard

3/4 cup hoisin sauce

1 4-pound pork tenderloin

1 1/2 cups water

2 cups light corn syrup

2 medium-sized red bell peppers, julienned

2 medium-sized green bell peppers, julienned

2 medium-sized yellow bell peppers, julienned

1 tablespoon chopped fresh cilantro

- Combine mustard and hoisin sauce to make marinade.
- Marinate pork in marinade for 6 hours.
- Combine water and corn syrup in large saucepan.
- Add peppers and cook until liquid is reduced to syrup consistency.
- Drain peppers to make pepper marmalade and reserve liquid. Set pepper marmalade aside at room temperature.
- Add cilantro to reserved liquid and pour mixture into cast-iron skillet.
- Drain marinade from pork and discard marinade.
- Place pork in skillet with cilantro mixture and cook over medium heat until all sides are caramelized well and pork is cooked to medium doneness (185 degrees on meat thermometer), approximately 30 minutes.
- Transfer pork to warm serving plate and allow to rest for 5 minutes.
- Serve pork with pepper marmalade.
- *Wine Suggestion:* Pinot Noir

Costolette di Agnello alla Griglia (Grilled Rack of Lamb)

Contributed by Griglio Toscana, courtesy of Former Mayor Daniel S. Frawley

Yield: 2 servings

¼ cup virgin olive oil

1 clove of fresh garlic, minced

Leaves of 1 sprig of fresh rosemary

Chopped fresh parsley to taste

1 rack of lamb, cut into 4 thick chops

Salt to taste

White pepper to taste

- Preheat grill or broiler.
- Heat oil in skillet.
- Sauté garlic in oil.
- Add rosemary and parsley just before garlic turns golden in color.
- Cool oil mixture.
- Season chops with salt and pepper, and coat each chop with oil mixture.
- Cook chops for approximately 3 minutes on each side or to your preferred doneness.
- Remove chops from heat, top with a little more oil mixture and serve.
- *Note:* Great for an elegant outdoor barbecue. Wonderful served with fresh vegetables and grilled polenta.
- *Wine Suggestion:* Chianti Classico

Rack of Lamb with Mustard-Peppercorn Crust

Contributed by The Back Burner,
Hockessin, Delaware

Yield: 3 servings

2 cloves of garlic, divided

1   7-rib rack of lamb,
    trimmed of all but ⅓ inch
    fat, chin bones cracked and
    bones Frenched

Lemon juice

Corn oil

Salt and pepper to taste

¾ cup white wine, divided

½ cup bread crumbs

½ cup chopped parsley

1 teaspoon chopped fresh
    rosemary

1 teaspoon chopped fresh thyme

1½ tablespoons crushed mixed
    white, black and green
    peppercorns

2 tablespoons Dijon mustard

5 tablespoons butter, softened,
    divided

½ cup lamb or beef broth

Fresh rosemary sprigs

- Preheat oven to 450 degrees.
- Split 1 garlic clove and rub over bone side of lamb. Discard garlic.
- Rub lamb with lemon juice, then oil. Heat skillet over medium-high heat and sear lamb on all sides.
- Place lamb in large roasting pan and sprinkle with salt and pepper.
- Cover each rib bone with foil to prevent burning.
- Add ¼ cup wine to roasting pan.
- Roast lamb for 20 to 25 minutes for rare or 25 to 30 minutes for medium. Mince remaining garlic.
- Preheat broiler.
- Combine garlic, bread crumbs, parsley, herbs, peppercorns, mustard and 1 tablespoon butter.
- Press crumb mixture firmly over fleshy part of lamb.
- Broil lamb, crumb side up, for 2 minutes or until lightly browned. Remove lamb from roasting pan.
- Skim fat from roasting pan, add remaining wine and boil down rapidly, stirring to deglaze pan.
- Add lamb broth, boil and strain to make sauce. Whisk remaining butter into sauce, heating until butter is melted.
- Carve lamb into individual chops, arrange on hot plates and top with sauce.
- Garnish with rosemary sprigs.
- *Wine Suggestion:*
  Cabernet Sauvignon

Veal Marengo

Contributed by Amalfi Restaurant, Greenville, Delaware

4 to 5 teaspoons olive oil, divided

1¾ pounds veal, cut into 1½-inch cubes

½ teaspoon salt

1 medium-sized onion, cut into 8 wedges

1   16-ounce can whole peeled tomatoes

¾ cup dry white wine

¾ cup water

2 cloves of garlic, minced

1 teaspoon thyme

¼ teaspoon pepper

2 cups button mushrooms or large mushrooms, quartered

1 tablespoon cornstarch

1 tablespoon cold water

Chopped parsley to taste

Yield: 6 servings

- Heat 3 to 4 teaspoons oil in Dutch oven or large saucepan over medium heat.
- Brown veal ½ at a time on all sides.
- Remove veal from pan, sprinkle with salt and set aside.
- Cook onion in remaining oil over medium heat until tender-crisp, about 3 to 4 minutes. Remove from pan and set aside.
- Return veal to pan.
- Add tomatoes with liquid to pan, breaking up tomatoes with spoon.
- Add wine and enough water to cover ingredients.
- Stir in garlic, thyme and pepper.
- Simmer, covered, for 45 minutes.
- Add mushrooms and onion.
- Continue cooking for 25 minutes or until veal and vegetables are tender.
- Dissolve cornstarch in cold water.
- Stir dissolved cornstarch into veal mixture and bring to a boil. Cook and stir until sauce is thickened and clear.
- Garnish with parsley.
- *Wine Suggestion:* French Beaujolais

Chicken Pomodoro

*Contributed by Caffè Bellissimo,
Wilmington, Delaware*

1 pound boneless chicken
  breasts

Flour for dredging

1 clove of fresh garlic

¼ cup olive oil

3 plum tomatoes, sliced

¼ cup sliced scallions

¼ teaspoon chopped fresh
  basil

1 cup white wine

¼ cup butter

8 ounces jumbo lump crab
  meat

½ cup shredded mozzarella
  cheese

Yield: 4 servings

- Preheat oven to 350 degrees.
- Wash chicken and pat dry.
- Dredge chicken in flour and sauté chicken and garlic in oil in large skillet until browned.
- Drain oil and remove chicken from skillet.
- Add tomatoes, scallions, basil, wine and butter to skillet and cook over medium heat to make sauce.
- Place chicken in 2-quart baking pan and top with crab meat and cheese.
- Bake for 5 minutes or until cheese is melted and lightly browned.
- Remove chicken to serving dish, top with sauce and serve.
- *Wine Suggestion:* Chardonnay

Chicken Diablo

*Contributed by The David Finney Inn,
New Castle, Delaware*

1 heaping teaspoon dry
  mustard

1 heaping teaspoon oregano

1 heaping teaspoon Cajun or
  Creole spice

¼ cup butter or margarine

1 whole chicken breast,
  skinned, boned and halved

Flour for dredging

3 plum tomatoes, sliced

1 cup beef broth

4 slices provolone cheese

2 cups fettucini or linguine,
  cooked according to
  package instructions and
  drained

½ cup chicken broth

Yield: 2 servings

- Combine mustard, oregano and
  Cajun spice. Set aside.
- Preheat large saucepan.
- Add butter to pan and allow to
  melt.
- Wash chicken and pat dry.
- Slice chicken into strips and
  dredge in flour.
- Add chicken to pan.
- Turn chicken over when half
  cooked, and add spice mixture
  to pan.
- Add tomatoes and beef broth to
  pan, lower heat and simmer until
  chicken is tender.
- Cover chicken with cheese slices
  and simmer until melted.
- Reheat pasta in chicken broth in
  separate saucepan.
- Drain pasta and place in serving
  dish.
- Serve chicken atop pasta.
- *Wine Suggestion:*
  California Zinfandel or
  Chenin Blanc

Stuffed Quail

Contributed by Constantino's Restaurant, Wilmington, Delaware

6 tablespoons olive oil

3 cloves of garlic, minced

14 quail

1   8-ounce can oysters

4 stalks celery, diced

2 tablespoons butter

1 teaspoon sage

Salt and pepper to taste

1 pound bread crumbs

Yield: 7 servings

- Combine olive oil and garlic. Pour over quail.
- Marinate quail in refrigerator overnight.
- Preheat oven to 350 degrees.
- Drain oysters. Reserve oyster liquid and set aside.
- Sauté celery in butter. Add oysters, sage, salt and pepper.
- Add bread crumbs gradually, mixing well until stuffing is slightly firm.
- Mix reserved oyster juice into stuffing and add more bread crumbs until very firm.
- Stuff quail with oyster stuffing.
- Place quail in buttered baking pan and bake for 20 minutes.
- Check joints of quail to ensure doneness and that meat has turned white.
- *Note:* Serve with wild rice.
- *Wine Suggestion:* California Chardonnay or Gamay Beaujolais

Roast Pheasant

Contributed by Wilmington Country Club, Wilmington, Delaware

Yield: 4 servings

1 2½-pound pheasant	⅓ cup chopped celery
Salt and pepper to taste	1 sprig of fresh thyme or pinch of dried thyme
¼ cup butter or margarine, divided	¼ cup Chambord, Cognac, port or flavored Brandy
1 bay leaf	1 cup crème fraiche
1 tablespoon chopped shallots	1 pinch of Jamaican allspice
⅓ cup chopped onion	1 cup fresh raspberries
⅓ cup chopped carrots	

- Preheat oven to 450 degrees.
- Season pheasant with salt and pepper. Truss with string to help keep its shape while cooking.
- Melt ½ of the butter over medium heat in cast-iron skillet or small roasting pan. Place pheasant in pan as butter begins to brown, and roll to coat on all sides. Leave pheasant on its side and place pan in oven.
- Bake pheasant approximately 12 minutes per pound turning pheasant over to other side halfway through baking.
- Remove from pan, let cool slightly, and remove legs and breast meat with knife. Keep meat warm.
- Break up carcass with scissors or large knife and return to pan. Add bay leaf, shallots, onion, carrots, celery and thyme and cook in pan drippings over medium heat for approximately 10 minutes.
- Add liquor and cook for 1 minute. Add crème fraiche and allspice, and simmer for another 3 minutes.
- Strain sauce through fine strainer into bowl, whisk in remaining butter, and season with salt and pepper.
- Breasts may be served whole or sliced thinly and arranged with the legs on platter or plates.
- Garnish with raspberries and sauce.
- *Note:* The drumstick of an adult pheasant leg is a bit tough and stringy and should not be served to guests.
- *Wine Suggestion:* Merlot

Brandywine Duck for Two

Contributed by The Waterworks Cafe, Wilmington, Delaware

1   4¹/₂ to 5-pound duck

1 cup wild rice

¹/₃ pound Italian summer sausage

1   10-ounce can mandarin oranges, undrained

1 cup orange juice

2 cinnamon sticks

¹/₄ cup packed brown sugar

¹/₄ cup Brandy

¹/₄ cup cornstarch

¹/₂ cup water

Yield: 2 servings

- Preheat oven to 375 degrees.
- Bake duck in roasting pan for approximately 1¹/₂ hours or until done.
- Cut duck into halves and partially debone.
- Cook rice according to package instructions.
- Brown sausage in large skillet.
- Combine undrained oranges and orange juice in medium saucepan and bring to a boil.
- Add cinnamon sticks, brown sugar and Brandy to saucepan, and boil for 3 minutes to form sauce.
- Combine cornstarch and water and add to sauce, stirring until thickened.
- Reheat duck until crisp.
- Place rice and sausage on serving plates and top with duck.
- Drizzle sauce over duck.
- *Wine Suggestion:* Alsacian Gewurztraminer

Flounder Français with Lemon-Garlic Cream Sauce

Contributed by The Granary Restaurant, Georgetown, Maryland

Yield: 1 serving

1 4-ounce flounder filet

Flour

1 egg, beaten

1 tablespoon butter

2 tablespoons white wine

¼ cup heavy cream

1 scallion, chopped

1 teaspoon chopped garlic

1 teaspoon lemon juice

Salt and pepper to taste

- Dredge flounder in flour, shake off excess, then dip into egg.
- Melt butter in small skillet and heat until very hot so that egg will cook as soon as it hits the pan without sticking.
- Sauté flounder in butter until browned on both sides. Drain off excess butter.
- Add white wine to deglaze pan.
- Add cream, scallion, garlic, lemon juice, salt and pepper.
- Cook over high heat for about 1 to 2 minutes or until reduced to sauce consistency.
- Place flounder on plate and cover with sauce. Serve hot.
- *Wine Suggestion:* Sauvignon Blanc

Baked Salmon Filets Briabe

Contributed by Lenape Inn,
West Chester, Pennsylvania

4 6-ounce salmon filets

½ pound small sea scallops

Fresh dill to taste

¼ pound Brie cheese, cut into
  strips

Yield: 4 servings

- Preheat oven to 350 degrees.
- Cut lengthwise incision halfway
  through each side of filets.
- Fill cuts in filets with scallops.
- Place filets in baking pan with a
  touch of water for moist baking.
- Sprinkle filets with dill.
- Bake for 8 minutes, remove
  from oven and place strips of
  Brie over filets.
- Bake for 4 to 7 minutes more.
- *Wine Suggestion:* Pouilly Fuissé

Bay Scallops Gruyère

Contributed by Hunter's Den
Restaurant, Wilmington, Delaware

¼ cup olive oil

2 pounds bay scallops

1 small onion, finely diced

½ pound mushrooms, sliced

3 ounces dry Sherry or white
  wine

1 teaspoon dill

1 teaspoon lemon pepper

2 medium-sized tomatoes, diced

½ pound Gruyère or Swiss
  cheese, grated

Chopped fresh parsley to taste

Yield: 6 servings

- Preheat oven to 350 degrees.
- Heat oil in large skillet and sauté
  scallops, onion and mushrooms
  until scallops are opaque. Drain.
- Add Sherry to skillet and
  simmer scallops and vegetables
  for 1 to 2 minutes. Add dill,
  lemon pepper and tomatoes and
  simmer for 1 minute more.
- Pour into one 2-quart or 6
  individual casserole dishes and
  top with cheese. Bake until
  cheese melts.
- Sprinkle with parsley.
- *Wine Suggestion:* Pouilly Fumé

Broiled Catfish with Asparagus and Thyme-Tomato Vinaigrette

Contributed by The Rodney Square Club, Wilmington, Delaware

Yield: 4 servings

4 6-ounce catfish filets	2 shallots, diced
2 tablespoons olive oil	1/2 tablespoon chopped fresh thyme
1/2 cup white wine	1/3 teaspoon pepper or 8 to 10 turns on a pepper mill
2 cups rice vinegar	
1 pound asparagus spears	
2 tomatoes	

- Trim filets, brush with olive oil, and place in ovenproof pan large enough to hold filets in one layer.

- Pour wine over filets, pour vinegar over filets, and refrigerate for 30 minutes.

- Blanch asparagus in boiling water for 4 to 5 minutes. Remove asparagus spears from hot water and plunge into ice-cold water immediately to keep crisp and green. Set aside.

- Blanch tomatoes for 1 minute in hot water used to blanch asparagus. Remove and plunge into ice-cold water. Peel tomatoes when cool, remove core and seeds, and chop pulp.

- Preheat broiler.

- Broil filets 4 to 5 inches from heat source for 8 to 10 minutes. Filets will become golden brown as sugar from rice vinegar caramelizes. Remove filets from pan and set aside.

- Pour juice from broiler pan into sauté pan.

- Add shallots and bring to a boil. Add thyme, tomatoes and pepper.

- Stir and remove from heat.

- Arrange asparagus and filets on warm serving plate and top with tomato mixture.

- Serve immediately.

- *Note:* A perfect low-calorie, low-cholesterol dish. Good when fresh asparagus is in season. Salmon, snapper, perch or similar fish filets may be substituted for catfish filets.

- *Wine Suggestion:* French Meursault

Angel Hair Pasta with Shiitake Mushrooms

Contributed by The Longwood Inn,
Kennett Square, Pennsylvania,
the mushroom capital of the world

Yield: 6 servings

¹/₃ cup vegetable oil

1 carrot, julienned

1 onion, julienned

2 green bell peppers, julienned

2 tablespoons sesame oil

¹/₂ pound shiitake mushrooms,
  sliced

4 ounces beef tenderloin,
  julienned

1 teaspoon chopped garlic

¹/₂ teaspoon chopped fresh
  ginger

2 teaspoons sugar

3 tablespoons soy sauce

10 ounces angel hair pasta,
  cooked according to
  package instructions,
  drained and cooled

- Heat vegetable oil in large skillet. Sauté carrot, onion and peppers until softened.

- Add sesame oil, mushrooms, beef strips, garlic, ginger, sugar and soy sauce to skillet.

- Sauté, stirring, until beef and mushrooms are tender.

- Add cooked pasta, stir well and serve.

- *Wine Suggestion:* Australian Shiraz

Penne Arrabiate

Contributed by Positano's,
Wilmington, Delaware

2 cloves of garlic, shaved

¼ cup olive oil

1 anchovy filet, finely
chopped

½ cup chopped fresh basil

½ pound penne, cooked
according to package
instructions and drained

1 cup marinara sauce

Grated Romano cheese to
taste

Yield: 4 servings

- Sauté garlic in oil in large skillet
  until browned.
- Add anchovy and basil to pan.
- Add pasta and cook until olive
  oil is absorbed.
- Add marinara sauce and toss.
- Garnish with cheese.
- *Wine Suggestion:*
  Italian Barbaresco

Risotto alla Principessa

Contributed by Griglia Toscana,
Wilmington, Delaware

1 pound Arborio (Italian
  short grain) rice

¼ cup olive oil

2 cups dry white wine, divided

2 cups chicken broth, divided

10 ounces shrimp, peeled and
  deveined

Diced shallots to taste

½ cup unsalted butter, divided

10 spears asparagus, blanched
  and sliced

½ cup clam juice

Juice of 2 lemons

½ cup grated Reggiano cheese

Yield: 4 servings

- Sauté rice in oil over medium-high heat in pan large enough to allow rice to triple in volume.
- Add ½ cup wine to rice and cook slowly until liquid is absorbed, stirring constantly.
- Add ½ cup chicken broth and cook until all liquid is absorbed.
- Continue alternating additions of wine and broth, allowing rice to completely absorb each addition. Maintain steady simmer to attain creamy, *al dente* texture.
- Sauté shrimp and shallots briefly in 1 tablespoon butter in large skillet.
- Add asparagus to skillet and continue to cook until shrimp turn pink.
- Add rice and clam juice to skillet and heat through.
- Add remaining butter to rice mixture and stir until melted.
- Add lemon juice and cheese to rice mixture and toss furiously.
- Serve immediately.
- *Wine Suggestion:* Italian Orrieto

Italian-Style Mushroom Casserole

*Contributed by Hugo's Inn,
Kennett Square, Pennsylvania,
the mushroom capital of the world*

2 large green bell peppers,
  seeded

1 pound blanched
  mushrooms, sliced

1 medium-sized onion, peeled
  and cut into rings or diced

½ cup oil or butter

1 cup homemade Italian
  tomato sauce

6 slices soft provolone cheese

Yield: 4 servings

- Cut peppers into ³/₄x1½-inch long strips.
- Sauté mushrooms, pepper strips and onion in oil until onion begins to lose whiteness.
- Place mixture into casserole dish.
- Pour Italian sauce over mixture and cover with cheese.
- Broil until cheese browns partially.
- *Note:* Serve with cold Italian bread slices and garlic butter.

Roquefort Bliss Potatoes

*Contributed by Concordville Inn,
Concordville, Pennsylvania*

32 red bliss potatoes

¼ pound Roquefort cheese

¼ cup heavy cream

1 egg

¼ cup fresh bread crumbs

1 pound jumbo lump crab
  meat

Yield: 8 servings

- Cut 1 end from potatoes to provide stable base.
- Hollow out potatoes from other end with melon scoop to form cup.
- Steam or boil potatoes for 5 minutes and cool in water.
- Preheat oven to 375 degrees.
- Combine cheese, cream, egg and bread crumbs in large bowl.
- Fold in crab meat gently.
- Stuff crab mixture into cooled potato cups.
- Bake for 15 to 30 minutes.

The Hotel duPont's Famous Almond Macaroons

Contributed by Hotel duPont, Wilmington, Delaware

Yield: 80 macaroons

1 cup plus 2 tablespoons sugar

21 ounces (about 2 cups) canned or packaged almond paste

4 large egg whites, lightly beaten

1/2 teaspoon vanilla extract

3 tablespoons water

- Preheat oven to 400 degrees.
- Beat together sugar and almond paste in bowl or food processor until blended.
- Beat in egg whites and vanilla until smooth.
- Transfer mixture to pastry bag fitted with 1/2-inch plain tip.
- Pipe 3/4-inch wide mounds 1 inch apart onto baking sheets lined with waxed paper.
- Let dough stand for 2 hours.
- Bake in middle of oven for 8 to 10 minutes or until macaroons are pale gold in color.
- Lift waxed paper gently and pour 3 tablespoons water between waxed paper and baking sheet.
- Let macaroons steam for 15 seconds to loosen, then transfer to rack to cool completely.

Chocolate-Almond Meringues

Contributed by The Rodney Square Club, Wilmington, Delaware

Yield: 7 dozen

1 cup chopped almonds

1½ ounces semisweet chocolate, chopped

½ cup baking cocoa

¼ cup all-purpose flour

1⅓ tablespoons instant dry coffee crystals

8 egg whites

Pinch of salt

2¾ cups confectioners' sugar

¾ teaspoon vanilla extract

⅓ teaspoon almond extract

- Preheat oven to 275 degrees.
- Combine almonds, chocolate, cocoa, flour and coffee in bowl and set aside.
- Beat egg whites at medium speed until frothy.
- Add salt to egg whites and beat at high speed until soft peaks form.
- Add confectioners' sugar 1 tablespoon at a time to egg whites, beating after each addition.
- Continue to beat until stiff peaks form.
- Fold in vanilla and almond extracts and cocoa mixture.
- Drop batter by tablespoonfuls 2 inches apart onto greased cookie sheet.
- Bake for 25 minutes or until dry in center.

Chocolate-Peanut Butter Pie

*Contributed by Greensleeves
Restaurant, Wilmington, Delaware*

1¾ cups chocolate wafer
  cookie crumbs

1 cup plus 3 tablespoons
  sugar, divided

5 tablespoons unsalted butter,
  melted

8 ounces cream cheese

1 cup creamy peanut butter

2 cups chilled heavy cream,
  divided

1 cup semisweet chocolate
  chips

Yield: 8 servings

- Preheat oven to 350 degrees.

- Blend crumbs, 3 tablespoons sugar and butter in bowl.

- Press crumb mixture onto bottom and side of 9-inch pie plate. Bake crust in middle of oven for 10 minutes. Let cool.

- Beat cream cheese and peanut butter in large bowl until smooth.

- Beat remaining sugar into peanut butter mixture until well combined. Set aside.

- Whip 1½ cups heavy cream in chilled bowl until it forms soft peaks. Fold ¼ of the whipped cream into peanut butter mixture.

- Fold in remaining whipped cream gently, but thoroughly.

- Mound mixture into prepared crust and chill pie, covered, for at least 4 hours to overnight.

- Heat remaining cream in 1-quart saucepan to boiling.

- Remove saucepan from heat and add chocolate chips, stirring until mixture is smooth.

- Let chocolate mixture cool for 15 to 20 minutes or until cool to the touch.

- Pour cooled chocolate mixture evenly over chilled pie. Chill for 30 minutes more or until chocolate mixture is set.

Bailey's Irish Cream-Chocolate Chip Cheesecake

Contributed by Greensleeves Restaurant, Wilmington, Delaware

Yield: 16 servings

2½ cups chocolate wafer cookie crumbs	1 cup sour cream
5 tablespoons butter, melted	4 teaspoons vanilla extract
2 pounds cream cheese, softened	7 tablespoons Bailey's Irish Cream
1 cup sugar	4 ounces semisweet chocolate, chopped
4 eggs	½ cup heavy cream

- Preheat oven to 275 degrees.
- Combine cookie crumbs and butter and press into 10-inch springform pan sprayed with nonstick cooking spray.
- Beat cream cheese with electric mixer until smooth, approximately 3 minutes.
- Add sugar and beat until well blended, occasionally stopping to scrape the bottom and side of bowl.
- Continue to beat, adding eggs 1 at a time until smooth.
- Add sour cream, vanilla and 6 tablespoons Bailey's Irish Cream and mix.
- Pour the mixture into prepared pan and place on cookie sheet.
- Bake for 1 hour and 15 minutes.
- Turn off oven and leave cheesecake in oven with door closed for another hour.
- Run knife around edge to depth of ½ inch to loosen cake and prevent cracking.
- Cool on rack to room temperature, then refrigerate overnight.
- Heat chocolate and cream over very low heat until chocolate is completely melted.
- Add remaining 1 tablespoon Bailey's Irish Cream and pour mixture through sieve over cheesecake.
- Refrigerate.
- *Note:* This cheesecake is best if allowed to come to room temperature before serving. For tidier looking slices, dip knife into hot water and wipe off before cutting each slice. May be made up to 48 hours in advance. Freezes well.

Heath Bar Cheesecake

*Contributed by Greensleeves
Restaurant, Wilmington, Delaware*

2 cups chocolate wafer cookie
  crumbs

¼ cup butter, melted

8 1³/₁₆-ounce Heath bars

1½ cups heavy cream, divided

2 tablespoons instant dry
  coffee crystals

24 ounces cream cheese

1 cup sugar

4 eggs

1 tablespoon vanilla extract

2 cups milk chocolate chips

Yield: 12 servings

- Preheat oven to 275 degrees.
- Combine cookie crumbs and butter and press into 9-inch springform pan. Refrigerate for at least 15 minutes.
- Chop Heath bars in food processor, set ½ aside, and sprinkle remaining ½ over crust.
- Heat ½ cup cream until just warm enough to dissolve coffee crystals, stir until dissolved and set aside. Beat cream cheese and sugar in a large bowl with electric mixer until blended.
- Beat in eggs 1 at a time.
- Add ½ cup cream, vanilla and coffee-cream mixture and blend until smooth.
- Pour into crust. Bake for 1 hour.
- Turn off oven and leave cheesecake in oven with door shut for another hour. Remove cheesecake from oven, cool on rack to room temperature, and then refrigerate.
- Combine chocolate chips and remaining cream in saucepan over low heat.
- Stir until melted and smooth.
- Cool to room temperature and pour over cooled cheesecake.
- Garnish with remaining chopped Heath bars.

Banana-Pecan Bread Pudding

Contributed by The Rodney Square
Club, Wilmington, Delaware   **Yield: 15 servings**

1 2-pound loaf French bread, cut into 2 inch cubes	1/2 cup packed light brown sugar
2 bananas, sliced	10 eggs
1 cup pecans	1 tablespoon vanilla extract
4 cups heavy cream	1/2 cup ginger Brandy
1/4 cup butter	1 tablespoon cinnamon
3/4 cup plus 2 tablespoons sugar, divided	Praline Whiskey Sauce (recipe follows)

- Preheat oven to 350 degrees.
- Fill buttered 9x13-inch baking pan with cubed bread.
- Add bananas and pecans to pan.
- Bring cream and butter to a simmer in large saucepan. Remove from heat.
- Add 3/4 cup sugar and brown sugar. Beat eggs with vanilla and Brandy. Add to cream mixture. Pour over bread.
- Cover with foil and bake for 20 to 25 minutes.
- Remove foil and sprinkle with remaining 2 tablespoons of sugar and cinnamon. Bake, uncovered, for 15 to 20 minutes more or until firm in center.
- Serve with warm Praline Whiskey Sauce.
- *Note:* Stale bread, raisin bread or croissants also work very well.

Praline Whiskey Sauce

2 cups heavy cream	1/2 cup whiskey
1/2 cup packed dark brown sugar	1 tablespoon arrowroot or cornstarch

- Bring heavy cream to a boil in saucepan.
- Add brown sugar.
- Mix whiskey with arrowroot and beat into cream mixture.
- Remove from heat.

Recipe Testers

The Cookbook Committee expresses its appreciation to League members and friends who gave of their time and talents by testing the recipes in this cookbook for accuracy and excellence.

Carol Harlan Aastad
Jill Abbott
Kristy Ambrogi
Patricia Antilla
Nancy Aronholt
Susan Asher
Julie Bartrum
Mitzi Beck
Keith Beddingfield
Margaret Begg
Sally Berbert
Charlene Bertheaud
Noreen Bowens
Sally Boyer
Jentje Cain
Michele Campbell
Sarah Cates
Barbara Chisholm
Harley Claffey
Deborah Cole
Katy Connolly
Pam Cornforth
Joan Crifasi
Betty Crowell
Amy Davis
Beth Day
Lee Ann Dean
Sandy Deckard
Cynthia deLeon
Diane DeLorenzo
Len deRohan
Mary Demmy
Julie Diebold
Sheila DiSabatino

Lonnie Dobbs
Karen Doherty
Mary Jane Donnelly
Emily Dryden
Susie Dunwody
Claudia Dunleavy
Kim Eastburn
Sherri Eastburn-Barkan
Donna Everson
Eileen Ferrell
Cabby Flynn
Amanda Foster
Susan Foster
Lynn Fuller
Beverley Fleming
Jill Gaumer
Meg Gehret
Joan Gehrke
Lori Gettelfinger
Paige Gilbert
Martha Gilman
Lisa Glover
Tina Golt
Sally Goodman
Sarah Goudy
Anne Gould
Mara Grant
Marjorie Grant
Stephanie Grant
Meredith Graves
Nancy Graves
Karen Green
Connie Greendoner
Cara Lee Grim

Ellen Hamilton
Becky Hamlin
Kathy Hancock
Mimi Harlan
Janis Harrison
Mary Hickok
Stephen Hillis
Monique Holloway
Sheila Holvech
Kathy Hopkins
Mary Ann Horning
Lisa Humphreys
Mary Humphrey
Jim Jaquin
Mady Jaquin
Maureen Kanara
Diane Keighley
Sheila Kern
Amanda Kimball
Harriott Kimmel
Sandy King
Hazel Kirk
Joann Kirk
Katherine Kolb
Doris Kremer
Pat Kremer
Susan Kremer
Diane Lawson
Karen Lazar
Karen LeBlond
Karen Leyden
Laura Lindsay
Julie Lowe
Franny Maguire

Tracey Martel
Jane Martin
Sally McBride
Barbara McCain
Maureen McCollom
Marjorie McGraw
Ann Moore
Meghan Moran
Peggy Morrell
Mary Ball Morton
Sisi Morris
Maud Mullen
Lisa Muller
Tracey Mulvaney
Kelly Nienhaus
Susan Nelson
Mary Ann Newcomb
Pat Nichols
Maria Nogle
Vicki Novak
Nancy Oberlin
Heather O'Connell
Anne O'Hara
Debbie Orga
Kerry Osborne
Mary Lu Pamm
Diane Paul
Sandy Pembleton

Kristi Pepper
Louise Perna
Carol Pyle
Dorothea Ragsdale
Barbara Reed
Marilyn Reukauf
Sharon Reuter
Mary Rice
Jenny Richardson
Laura Robelen
Sharon Rolle
Becky Rosen
Sharon Rothwell
Andrea Rotsch
Cathy Scanlon
Pat Scully
Kathy Segars
Lynette Shawd
Shirley Shepherd
Jill Sheridan
Eliza Shicktanz
Angie Sigmon
Jenny Simonton
Kim Simpson
Mary Ann Slovin
Pat Smith
Nina Sneeringer
Judy Sonnett

Barbara Sowden
Mimi Sparks
Mona Sparks
Linda Tabeling
Debbie Talbert
Anne Taylor
Nancy Tieste
Cathy Timmons
Cindy Thompson
Martha Tshantz
Mary Vane
Sally Van Orden
Christina Veith
Mary Vollendorf
Beth Ann Wahl
Moira Walker
Kearsley Walsh
Carolyn Wells
Jean Western
Carla Williamson
Susan Williams
Mary Jean Wilson
Pam Witsil
Diane Wood
Virginia Wood
Michelle Wright
Darragh Zehring
Donna Zinnato

Index

Index

Notes

Notes